W9-BGN-256

Backyard Birding in the Northeast United States

Backyard Birding in the Northeast United States

Elmer Waldemar Eriksson

LAST POST PRESS

Falls Village, Connecticut

An imprint of

SEVEN LOCKS PRESS

Santa Ana, California
Minneapolis, Minnesota
Washington, D.C.
Helena, Montana

Seven Locks Press
P.O. Box 25689
Santa Ana, CA 92799
(800) 354-5348

Individual Sales. This book is available through most bookstores or can be ordered directly from Seven Locks Press at the address above.

Quantity Sales. Special discounts are available on quantity purchases by corporations, associations, and others. For details, contact the "Special Sales Department" at the publisher's address above.

Printed in the United States of America

Library of Congress Cataloging-in-Publication Data
Eriksson, Elmer Waldemar, 1932-
Backyard birding in the Northeast United States / Elmer Waldemar Eriksson.
p. cm.
ISBN 1-931643-04-0 (pbk.)
1. Bird-watching—Northeastern States. 2. Bird feeders—Northeastern States.
3. Birdhouses—Northeastern States. 4. Birds--Food—Northeastern States. 5. Birds--Feeding and feeds—Northeastern States. I. Title.
QL676.5.E768 2002
598'.07'23474—dc21

2002000300

Cover and Interior Design by Sparrow Advertising & Design

Dedication

Dedicated to my wife, Audrey, my typist, who accompanied me on all craft shows for twelve years and will corroborate every word in this book as true and accurate.

Also to both of my sons, Bret and Mark, who helped us in many different ways.

Table of Contents

Foreword

Birds on the wing, peeking from a cavity or perching on a branch, appeal to the interests and affection of most people. Graceful forms, harmonious colors, sprightly actions, and delightful songs always draw our attention and deep interest. All birds in flight intrigue us, and we follow their movement.

In our time, the way to birding is to attract them to your grounds with a good feeder, or even several feeders placed outside a window, and watch them alight.

Backyard birding has become a popular outdoor hobby. For some time now, I feel it should be much more substantial as a part of the garden and landscape in the nation. It can be close to a religious experience. There are the window watchers in birding, which includes most people.

Because the trees in most of the East have closed in on us, open residential areas can make the difference to cavity-nesting species with birdhouses to specification and larger barn feeders with a good supply of seed. Being generous with seed in winter assures survival. The chickadee, of course, always shows up and even feeds out of your hand, if you're patient.

The pressure of population regiments us so that we are closer together. Gardens, and especially the bird garden, can fill a need for contact with nature. Birds on your feeder are seen daily as free, unrestrained, and unafraid.

Appendix C, Community Bird Refuges by W. L. McAtee, is a sampling out of the past of how people thought about birds early in the twentieth century. It is a bit earthier than present perspectives and makes for an interesting comparison.

This book takes us through the window and into a suburban or rural backyard or private estate.

These guidelines are a big step forward for the birder and result from my years of building birdhouses.

Preface

Much of this book on backyard birding is based on my twelve years of hands-on experience in constructing and selling custom birdhouses and bird feeders. I started off with bluebird houses, but I soon realized there was little artistic integrity in a "box" when, with rural America as a guide, a birdhouse or a bird feeder could be constructed as a landscape complement and not just the functional box that worked well on many bluebird trails.

The look I was after was based on early barns, outbuildings, and homes in rural America; that is, original designs that manifested integrity, form, and function. With a barn, bench, tools, and shelves, I started with bluebird and clay flowerpot houses and evolved ideas as to what form birdhouses and bird feeders should be. (Eric Sloane's book on farm structures was a great help.) I gradually found sources for all types of weathered wood and a variety of barn siding, and I even went up into Vermont to purchase pure slate from a quarry to use as roofs on very special feeders and houses.

The standard American birdhouse and feeder is an ideal accoutrement for every home. Prior to 1950 and the arrival of mass- produced products, the standard birdhouse was rural and rustic in expression and individually handcrafted. It was this handcrafting that made this nation great. The hand-builder of birdhouses really starts from the inside, using quoted dimensions. However, what happens on the outside is an expression of the craftsman, and this is where his real interest lies.

The birdhouses and feeders in photos represent a rural American standard in design and finish. They are a new/old standard that anticipates a move to a more traditional and poised landscape based on the land (i.e., a different use other than those known on the roadways, at the malls, or in shopping centers). Regardless of our current global economy, people do have their feet planted firmly on the ground and want that to be known. Nature is a consistent standard, and handcrafting is a natural art in origin and inspiration. These handcrafted designs anticipate that people really know their "organic" roots. It is the beauty of the exterior covering of all things that affects the mind, while the activities in the birdhouse are entirely private and for the birds.

In my part of Connecticut, there are many antique dealers, and I can find many old birdhouses and feeders. They are charming, to say the least, and with a drill and appropriate screws to replace rusty loose nails, and with some polyurethane, stain, paint, or antiquing, you can have a gem for the next fifty or more years. You can even replace old hinges and hooks and even polyurethane the bare wood roof. Nothing needs to be done on the inside.

Do right by the birds.

We may as well get down to brass tacks in America and celebrate birds as worth our time and effort. Our economy and helter-skelter way of life have wreaked havoc on the land and for winged creatures. My guess is that, short of a miracle, agriculture is going to stay static for the foreseeable future. The miracle might be the return to small-scale agriculture based on state-by-state or region-by-region needs. Our situation now is that there is a shortfall numbering in the millions of natural cavities in trees compared to 1900–1950. If the trees and forests are not there to provide cavities, the cavity nesters are endangered. If, as in crop monoculture, seed-bearing grasses and berry-bearing shrubs and trees are absent, the bird species that depend on these will suffer. My main motive for writing this book is that, as a nurseryman and landscape designer, I've come to see the new American landscape design as both horticultural and ornithological: a beautiful place for people and a feeding habitat that birds can use throughout the year.

A variety of barn feeders on display

CHAPTER I

Sustainable Bird Ecology

Even the oldest of villages are indebted to the border of wild-woods which surround them more than to the gardens of men.

—Henry Thoreau

As a boy in Fairfield, Connecticut, I remember the great numbers of birds and insects that lived here for many a summer. Now I know the birds were supposed to be there to control the insects and to control the seeds from weeds, all according to nature's needs.

The number of birds in the environment of Connecticut is much less than forty-five to fifty years ago. In 1950, there were many more farms offering all the advantages that open fields offer birds. Birds are with us only as long as there is food for them. Their main preoccupation is survival and procreation, and all creatures are good at these things when food is available. When farms were in abundance, there were hedgerows and cornfields and sunny open areas. This allowed many berry- and seed-bearing plants to yield their bounty as well as seed from many species of grass plants. In this sunny environment, insects flourished and older trees provided many cavities for cavity-nesting birds. The wild songbirds did exceptionally well in these ideal conditions.

In the past fifty years, many farms were abandoned or sold. Pastures grew back to forests and the ground was soon completely shaded. As this happened, less square miles of land in the Northeast were in sunlight and provided fewer berries, fruit, seeds, and insects.

The birds' natural habitat disappeared a long time ago. Open land is required for them to remain, now that forests that provide too much shade have displaced agriculture.

Another large problem is pollution from the ubiquitous automobile. As a grower of nursery stock, I know that the annual growth of trees in Connecticut is down by 25 percent due to auto exhaust emissions. I'm certain that all life-forms are affected by these emissions, including birds. Pollution must be minimized because people need birds as well as trees, shrubs, and lawns. Unfortunately, modern technology has weaned us from our earthly plantation. The thin skin of the earth's soil/atmosphere is our only abode in all space. We are abandoning the earth by not educating ourselves about its life, ecology, soil, water, and atmosphere.

While professing concern for the environment, the public consensus has been indifferent at best. Except for landscape architects/designers, not too many people can comprehend the landscape of the nation. The total landscape or environment in America is on the decline, due in large part to urban development. Indifference to landscape probably means indifference to birds—I tend to read it that way. The wild songbirds, by many estimates, are fewer and fewer. The pervasive attitude is, "Don't feed the birds in the summer—let them browse for themselves," and this couldn't be further from the truth. In fact it is akin to saying, "Don't put up birdhouses, they'll find something." They won't!

This type of indifference is plainly ignorant, demonstrating that modern man has shown little affinity for landscape and garden. No public support for the traditional planned landscape in America probably underlies this state of general apathy toward birds and the traditional bird garden. As urban culture rises, culture of the natural diminishes with little observable evidence of a reversal.

Backyard birding may be a way to restore the wild songbird to prominence in every town and city. Even in the wild, birds are where they are because there is a ready food supply. If there isn't any food, they depart. Obviously, homeowners who love birds and understand that their natural habitat has been changed will be willing to operate feeders on a year-round basis. Backyard birders attract the wild birds to their backyards and the experience reaps rich rewards. The backyard feeding station is an important step toward compensating them for their difficult ecology and supplementing their diet. As with people, it is ultimately our social responsibility to provide food and housing in consideration of the bird's privilege to be here. In ecology, this responsibility is called community—or more to the point, bird ecology—the subject of this book. Our respective places in the environment preceded the economy which has negatively impacted bird habitats. The world is a magnificent bounty and the birds, as evolved, are entitled to their place in the sun alongside man. The course of landscape and garden brought men to nature and civilization, while the spirit of one mind saturates the atmosphere of our earth evolving all ecological systems. Natural systems must prevail, simply because there aren't any alternatives.

Large barn feeder on post

Birdhouses are as important as feeding stations. They should have a uniform design and be constructed of cedar, pine, or barn wood. I tell my customers that birdhouses work, if not one year, then the next. They are an ecological adjunct that is necessary and done as inconspicuously as possible. All people have success with them and when they experience the success, they put up others. I have spoken to over a thousand people who, on average, have three

Chickadee and clay-pot feeder

birdhouses. If an average of 25 to 50 percent is occupied, then that's a satisfactory number of housed birds. (Curiously, even though a number of ladies want a birdhouse, they say their husbands don't know how to put one up!)

I personally have a strong affinity for the land and agriculture. No creature should be denied its right for a place in ecology as formed by God. God has unlimited perception and understands the ecology of earth. The simple fact that God's nature evolved the wild songbird should be adequate evidence that they have an essential role in an ecology that no man should violate. People in agriculture know this and instinctively put up birdhouses.

Birdhouse have a long history of success, going back to their use (on a large scale by the USDA) as insect control projects. The love of nature was well expressed in the natural landscape of the American home of the 1950s when the estate feeder and birdhouse were common sights. More people must realize that supplemental feeding of wild birds is necessary and that nest boxes are required for two to three nestings annually. The only way to make amends to the birds for the destruction or altering of their environment is through our generosity with seed, houses, and water.

Bird ecology falls under the category of permanent ecology. As agriculture departs and forests grow back, bird ecology is a very descriptive phrase that describes the plight of all birds in finding habitat and food over vast regions. Ecology for the wild songbirds depends on individual people and their role in understanding the place of the bird in the microhabitat of the individual home. Bird ecology in America could best be thought of as a slightly or highly modified hedgerow that acts as a permanent buffer and is, therefore, husbanded accordingly.

Sustainable ecology for the birds is the same as for all God's plants and animals. Only by conforming to the real world in agriculture, the environment, landscape design, and the private home garden, can we force the issues into a new vernacular and rise up with our sustainable ecological ethic. This all ties in with a larger picture of sustainable ecology for the birds in the vast northeastern United States.

The way to accomplish or bring about a sustainable ecology for all is to restore the human landscape as it was in the1950s and, in effect, plan for people and birds, similar to what landscape architects and nurserymen did early on in the twentieth century. Change in environment means returning to a more sensible time. A sustainable ecology for all includes songbirds. The rationale is simple: a good step-by-step means to entice the birds with good horticulture and good landscape design that benefits for everyone.

CHAPTER 2

Bird Feeders and Feeding Stations

In the Northeast, we live in a world blessed with an abundance of flora and fauna. The seasons rotate, symbolizing the unending pattern of life. And yet, in the ecology of the migratory and nonmigratory songbirds, the patterns of land development, land use, and landscaping of the past fifty years or so have had a negative effect on the supply of food sources for all birds.

In our history, birds were given a great advantage when much of the East was cleared of trees and the land shaped for agriculture. To birds, this was the opening of a new world of plenty. There would be grain, weed seeds, insects, fruits, and berries. Agriculture created an Eden for the birds.

In the past forty years, however, land values have risen, and the uses for the land have changed radically from the ideal of agriculture to land development in many forms. It is written in natural law that all creatures have a need for shelter, food, freedom, and its accompanying joy. The natural abundance of food that is required for the songbird's sustenance and nesting cycle is not being met, as land is slowly being converted from

A multiple seed feeder (5)

Typical barn feeder

agriculture to residential or industrial uses. Bear in mind that farmland provided for birds in all ways. Bear in mind also what a boon land, shaped to the uses of agriculture, has always been. Like the birds, we are living in a second-rate environment as well. Fortunately, we can have our food shipped in; therefore the same must be done for birds in the form of seed for the backyard bird feeder.

Supplemental feeding in the winter is essential for the well-being of the birds during this critical period because the lives of many are at stake. As the frontiers in birding were in New England, so should a new frontier begin in the peace and seclusion of a backyard bird garden that will give us new experiences and perspectives on birds and the human environment.

We live on a natural schedule. However, Washington and the economy place us all in peril. When we simplify our feeders and nesting boxes and create true garden art rather than accept the hardware store gimcrackery, a significant change will take place in how we look at nature and the environment. Certainly, the use of such outlandish plastic contrivances and junk that are sold to supply birds with seed is every bit as objectionable in concept as prolific land development, malls, parking lots, atmospheric pollution, and non-environmental modern architecture. No economy can supersede the very nature that evolved all of us—it's not possible. Simply put, we adjust to nature.

Contemporary feeders are like much of modern architecture: made of plastic and wired together. And from what I have heard from countless people, they're more of a nuisance than anything else. My personal taste tells me that even the birds might harbor suspicions as for their personal safety with these plastic feeders that seem to intrude in the yard rather than fit into the environment. To those who have an interest in the garden and in many ways our environment, plastic (in any of its forms) is positively out of place. Plastic symbolizes in many ways the artifice of mankind holding us in a trance of change—possibly, for unknowing consumers, a very unnecessary change, or at least a change in an unpleasant direction. Eventually, people see "change" as ragtag and its form as representing the less noble side of man, the urban manufactory: much profit, but no substance of God, soil, and the green plant. Why? Probably because these things of nature don't come in a package at a discount or in a baker's dozen. Put another way, a chickadee metabolism cannot be duplicated by men or any computer program.

The "things" of man cannot replace the green plant and bird habitat. I am dazzled by the colors, forms, and songs of the birds; their faces and agility; their behavior at our feeders. I am aware that the birds are not aware of the design and that their main concern is for the availability of seeds. Even so, a feeder can be designed to accommodate the birds in seed capacity and convenience and also enhance the aesthetics of the yard. Therefore, we should always move toward the development of the American aesthetic.

Old carriage house wood made this unique small feeder.

Birds need the seed to be dry, and they happily accept communal feeding. When barn feeders are of a large dimension, they simply accommodate more birds and more seed at one time. The enthusiasm of the birds for seed that is offered to them in a barn feeder is heartening. The aspects of the barn feeder are essentially rural in origin and so the concept is traditional, while the construction is new and more sound than commercial feeders. Barn feeders, when well-placed with a small tree ten feet away for perching and waiting, provide the natural situation for songbirds. Placing a copper roof on the top will ensure that a leaping squirrel will simply slide off. Put on an inverted cone, and the climbing squirrel will be stopped.

Given the great disparity in the selection of bird feeders and how they affect the human psyche, a standard overall design that fits into the American garden should be given preference for the sake of encouraging simplicity and practicality. The barn feeder is by far the most pragmatic and aesthetically satisfactory feeder when we want seeds to be tasteful and dry. Great variety in mass-produced plastic and wooden seeders mostly creates a distraction instead of re-creating nature. *Keep it rustic.*

If you want to be a benefactor to the birds, feed them well. The overall dimensions of barn feeders vary in width, length, and height. The dimensions from the roofline to the horizontal bar is four to five inches and often higher for larger birds. Once a feeder is mounted, it is very easy to hang a food stick or suet cage on the end or both ends.

Having a wide roof means that seed and table scraps will stay dry and fresher longer than seed that is put out in open trays and subjected to the changing weather. In providing a suitable size feeder, your backyard will become a haven of migratory and nonmigratory species that are seedeaters. An important consideration is that the feeder be placed in an open area for easy access and departure. Birds need a full view around the feeder. Our feeder has always been four feet from the picture window and twelve feet from a weeping cherry tree. This seems to be a good arrangement. The cherry tree serves as a perch or waiting area.

Keep in mind that the barn feeder is critical to the function of an efficient feeding station in that it provides a mechanism that displays the seed in a manner that is hospitable to the birds and serves their

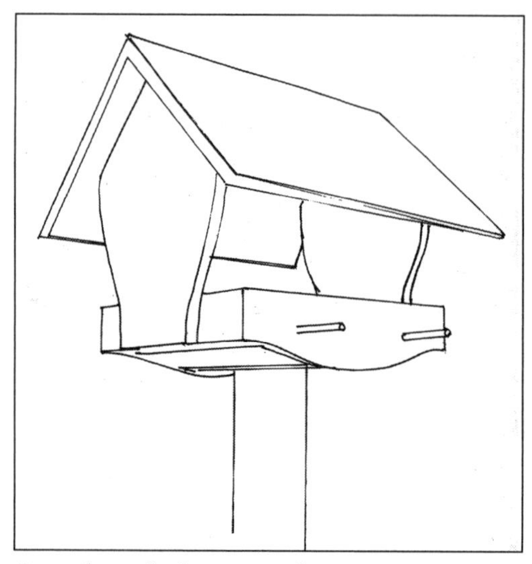

Large barn feeder on wooden post

convenience first and foremost. Protecting seed and table scraps from the weather extends palatability and nutritional value. The barn feeder actually evolved from the estate feeder that stood out in the rain and snow and prevented seed and table scraps from becoming rancid and moldy. As the birds are often repulsed by wet food, this has been the barn feeder's chief advantage.

The attendance numbers at our feeder is very high during the winter season. Usually, there are up to 100 to 200 visits through the day of purple finches, chickadees, nuthatches, juncos, and titmice. Other species that have visited us have been less in number and include cardinals and blue jays. The greatest number of birds at one time is in the early morning when their need for food is greatest. Imagine their energy requirements after roosting out in the cold on a typical winter's night. Barn feeders provide all the hospitality birds need to recover from cold nights. They also provide easy access and departure and excellent visibility. Many backyard birders maintain a large feeder with sunflower seeds, and several smaller feeders with thistle and white millet or combinations of seed known to attract specific birds. This is definitely something with which to experiment. Hang small feeders from corners or under the main feeder. Allow yourself some time to gain experience and work with nature's endless patience.

Barn feeders can be made of western cedar, white pine, cherry, mahogany, eastern red cedar, white cedar, or redwood. I prefer American white pine because it is native to the East and its history in house construction is well known. It weathers into a rural structure and responds to paint, stain, and polyurethane, adding to its charm and extending an attitude.

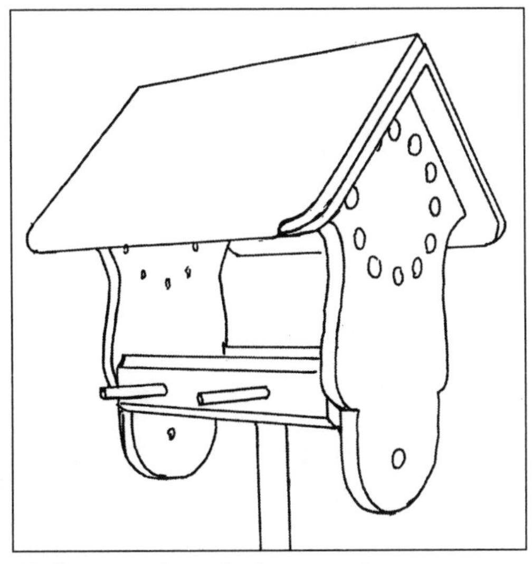

Medium-size barn feeder on a pipe

White pine is available in a full one-inch thickness. With the appropriate use of nontoxic wood preservatives, bird feeders should last for many years. Barn siding is being used more and more to build feeders. It is my feeling that feeders should be considered as garden art and styled to reflect the region's authentic history. Certainly, the history of estate feeders tells us that the roof is best preserved under several coats of oil paint, varnish, or polyurethane. Feeders are an extension of your home, garage, and barn, and should be designed accordingly.

Driving winds will occasionally bring in snow, or rain, but not enough to affect feeding habits or create a moldy condition. Barn feeders of all designs have the most square inches under a roof, so there is plenty of usable space for seed and feeding. The barn feeder, known in the past as an "estate feeder" provides many square inches of floor space and different depths allowing for more seed. One feeder might hold a week's supply of different seed.

Feeder complex

Variations on a theme on barn feeders are many. "Variations" mean to come up with adjunct smaller feeders available at garden and bird stores and attached in various ways to offer a wider variety of seed. The estate feeder of the past was a great step in offering and protecting seed. They were probably designed by landscape architects and cabinetmakers for use in gardens and were appropriate for the environment and any site for which they were selected. These feeders have glass hoppers that hold the seed. The barn feeder is patterned after a barn, but it has the advantage of seeing the birds on both sides, which means better visual accessibility to the birds and, with a solid roof overhead, protection from raptors and inclement weather. A large barn feeder, placed outside a favorite window, will have many visitors all through the day.

Bird-Feeding Stations

Bird-feeding stations are more complicated than a barn feeder. These stations hold from three to seven types of seed in a variety of trays. A suet cage or two can be fastened to the gable ends. Offering that many selections results in many different birds arriving at your feeder for their seed of preference. You will gather your own information on what type of feed will attract what type of bird. Be patient, and the birds will arrive in their own time . . . days to weeks. Also, be consistent in filling feeders with the same seed. A wide variety of birds are exactly what the backyard birder wants to see. A good variety of seeds and table scraps will accomplish this goal. Bird-feeding stations are large, which shows that the owner is earnest in this endeavor. An owner of a feeding station will soon take birding seriously.

A working feeding station will prove to be encouraging, and interest levels will increase the most practical way to attach yourself to nature. Plastic tubes and small feeders are inadequate and have never been an appropriate next step to higher levels of interest.

The placement of barn feeders and feeding stations is important. An open area is ideal and yet they can be placed only five to six feet from a window. Much depends on the local squirrel population. To prevent pilfering, galvanized, plastic, and copper baffles have been used. Ornithologists have recommended axle grease and the ointment Ben-Gay be applied to the pole holding the feeder. Mixing some cayenne pepper with the seed seems to work well. Two ladies I spoke with had each trapped fifteen squirrels and then took them to a state forest and released them. I have also heard of a lady who called an insect exterminator who trapped them. I guess, to some people, squirrels are a great problem, while others would just as soon feed them. Solutions are up to the individual. Barn feeders and feeding stations found in this book are an adaptation of estate feeders

Barn feeder

observed over many years in private gardens. At that time, they were rudimentary in function and design. That hasn't changed.

Some sixty million people in the United States are involved in backyard bird feeding. This certainly attests to the high level of interest and the concern of humans regarding birds and, in time, this interest will increase. Greater understanding of its rewards will draw more people to it as a hobby that converges with life on the land, and it coaxes people outside into the "bird garden" . . . the new American garden.

There are excellent reasons for sixty million people feeding birds. Nothing matches the untamed beauty of nature with a feeder in close proximity—just don't move too much. Be still and watch. Your birding skills will increase with continued observation. Roger Tory Peterson's *Field Guide to Birding* will be used a great deal to better identify the species that will appear.

The antics and movements of birds will fascinate you to no end! They will entertain you as you grow accustomed to their presence. How else can you see wild songbirds so close up, but with a barn feeder or feeding station? If you help the birds with supplemental feed, they will reward you with their presence! Think of it as a home study course in bird identification and a bird count of unusual species—real on-the-job training. Keep Peterson's books and other bird identification books on hand. Keep a list of the birds you see in a book—and keep the feeder full!

A diversity in bird species in your yard depends upon a diversity of food offerings, whether it be seeds or table scraps. The main feeder should hold a variety of sunflower seeds, while the smaller, attached feeders should hold a good supply of different seed types. Fruit spikes and peanut butter cups can be hung or fastened. A substantial feeding station can have many types of seed dispensers attached in ingenious ways; you're limited only by your imagination.

A bluebird house can be converted to a feeder that hangs on a post or against a house by removing the front and then fastening a horizontal piece of wood across the bottom to hold the seed in, which makes it barnlike, dry, and easy to move in; several of these converted birdhouses can hang from a feeder to add different types of seed. Many people and organizations have made tens of thousands of bluebird houses. They make good barn feeders and adjunct feeders by simple modification and a screw to attach them to a main feeder or a pole.

In many cases, a ten- to twelve-inch board, with a raised edge around the outside to hold the seed in, can be fastened outside a window. This makes supplying seed and scraps easy by just opening the window. In seasonal weather, it is still practical to maintain a platform groundfeeder, which is a platform feeder, but off the ground by six inches or so. This satisfies the preferences of actual ground feeders, like the doves, cardinals, and juncos. Often, it is a piece of wood screwed to a cutoff tree trunk or mounted on a 4 × 4 a foot above the ground.

Examine feeders at stores and make your own. Use galvanized screws and no nails. Good designs for your feeder can be easily built from studying the photos of barn feeders in this book and copying them directly, or adapting them to your own station needs. You can almost gauge the sizes from the photographs. The possibilities for design are endless as long as there is a covering of seed and easy access.

Because the outdoor cat is credited with fifty bird kills annually, an important consideration about a feeding station is NO CATS.

Conclusion

In the large environment of the Northeast, longtime pollution affects the yield of seed- and fruit-bearing trees and shrubs in comparison to fifty years ago. Insects, of course, are leaf eaters, and suckers and their numbers are down. Supplementing wild birds with seed all year long is necessary. It provides the best nutrition prior to the nesting season.

A year's experience with feeders will put you in good stead. This is the best teacher. In all of agriculture and horticulture, shelter, such as barns, sheds, greenhouses, and cold frames, are absolutely essential. These structures provide protection from the elements and work very well at protecting and sheltering animals and feed. Considering how we have changed the environment from an agrarian economy in which the songbirds benefited for several centuries (and, in effect, became our dependents), and for which they kept down insects to a tolerable amount, we are all obliged to give serious thought to providing them with generous backyard supplemental feeding structures.

Our economy created a problem nature could not anticipate. Creation is at the mercy of the unnatural and abstract phenomenon called money which, used well and wisely, would have avoided creating problems for the wild birds. In uncontrolled development, however, it isn't being used well at all.

Bluebirds feeding on mealy worms (courtesy Florence Sands)

Church birdhouse

Triplex of birdhouses; small, medium, and large with Vermont slate for roofs

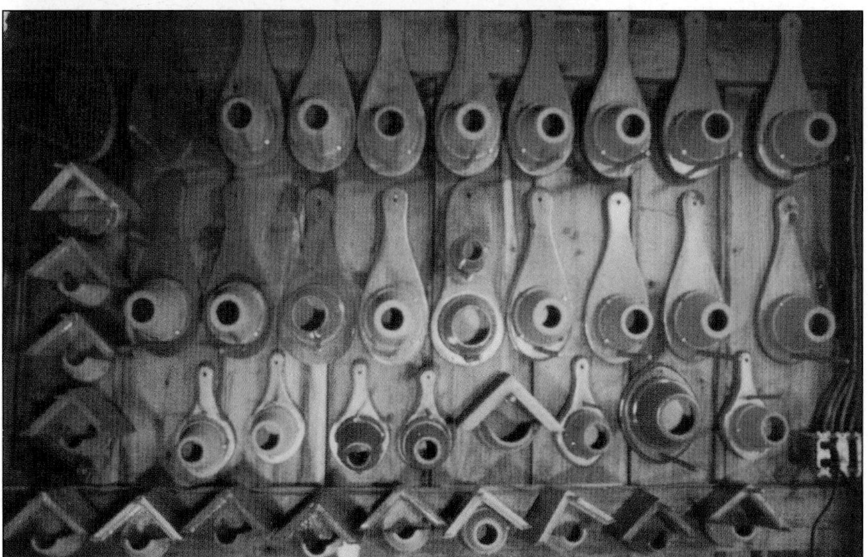

Clay flowerpots as feeders and nesting sites

Male bluebird

Male cardinal

(Used by permission from Cornell Orinthology, Cornell University, Ithaca, NY

Downy woodpecker

Blue jay

Rustic birdhouses at craft show display

Large barn feeder with a hanger for different seed, etc.

Bluebirds—parents and fledglings

CHAPTER 3

Bird Food

As the chickadee said to the titmouse in my feeder the other day, "This is for the birds!"

Man's harmonic cohabitation with birds came closest to perfection when people settled on the land and began to grow grain. At threshing time, the birds came closer and closer to man and took advantage of this easily attainable food source. After many years, the birds began to take the farm and farmer for granted as dependable sources of food. The birds also kept the insect population down. How many times have I seen birds at threshers and barn doors, and even inside the barn itself, foraging for seed? As bread is the staff of life for man, plump seed is the staff of life for many birds.

Thanks to ornithologists, we are leaps and bounds beyond scattering food and seed in the driveway. Luring wild birds to your garden and grounds brings a delight in sound, sight, and color few other activities can match. It would be a fair guess that untold millions in America feed the songbirds during all of the seasons. Of course, food from the feeder is only to supplement the natural diet of the birds. A well-stocked feeder brings them into the yard and provides suet and seed that, especially in winter, help the birds immensely. Drawing a large variety of birds takes an equally great variety of seeds and a variety of leftover table scraps diced into small pieces. The information in this chapter is drawn from what successful bird-feeding people have actually told me.

It seems that the birds in winter will eat anything, provided it is diced into quarter-inch pieces. In late winter, even bluebirds will come to your feeder if you have a mixture of raisins, peanut butter, and cornmeal suet (a protein-rich food important at times when insects are not plentiful). Check out sources of mealy worms.

I spoke with an elderly lady who chops up every bit of her leftover food into little bits and the birds take it all. I suggested that adding sunflower seeds would bring even more birds. Those who provide the few simple facilities for food, shelter, and water, to birds that may be under environmental stress, will be rewarded with a host of lively and chirping visitors as a daily event that could well become a lifelong project.

I have found that most people who are serious birders are putting out seed all year long. There is a growing awareness that in the disrupted and stressed environment of farms and forests of the northeastern United States there is not an adequate supply of insects. The migratory and nonmigratory birds are natural associates in the ecology of the yards and grounds of American homes. (I like to think of them as associates rather than neighbors.) They are a spectacular form of life—they fly so beautifully, catch and keep down the insect population, eat weed seeds, and are delightful to have around. In addition to being beautiful and useful, some are well known for their vocal abilities. They are true musicians and feathered friends, (for example, the house wren).

Like the green trees, the birds belong. What vegetation cannot supply in berry and seed, the backyard feeder can supplement. The feeding and social habits of a variety of seed-eating birds at our barn feeder on a year-round schedule is a matter of great interest. After awhile, we get to know the birds as individuals. In our case, a large feeder is four feet from a bay window and just about in the middle, so some three hundred chickadees, nuthatches, house finches, titmice, winter wrens, blue jays, and cardinals are back and forth constantly. What better way is there to bring the wild songbirds to your eye than a barn feeder and a mixture of seed for all the birds?

Because birds are shy and timid creatures, it is difficult for humans to get very close. Of course, just outside your home or in the wild, you can see them with binoculars. The way to know them is to feed them faithfully with a nutritious repast of easily available seed, suet, and table scraps. A garden is a very intense and artistic use of plant material, and every garden is a potential bird garden with a little revision. The greatest change you can make is to erect a pole with a feeder on top in your garden. The ideal bird garden would be designed by a landscape architect and would include berry trees and shrubs that have a high yield for fall and winter feeding. Also, a well-planted garden would attract a variety of insects who would be there for the garden's cover and then their own feeding. Trees and shrubs provide perching cover and nesting sites, and if there are dense evergreens, protection from both natural enemies and the weather. We have total dependence on plants; they are the basis of our ecology.

The formula for attracting many birds is simple: Keep the feeder filled with a variety of seeds. Actually, that means you must get some experience with the birds in your area over a period of time. A bit of experimentation will produce great results. I have descriptions of seed combinations given to me by hundreds of people, while they sound contradictory, really aren't. Experiments at Cornell show black oil sunflower seed, milo, and millet to be the favorite in the East. If you stick with that combination, you should do well. However, there are many seeds that have been used for a long time and are known to attract specific species and, in this sense, a period of trial and error is unavoidable. Long-term experience, however, is that sunflower seeds are the overwhelming favorite of the wild songbirds.

Farmers who originally grew the seed for human use gained what is known about bird preferences in seed. Crows, sparrows, grackles, and blackbirds would descend on corn and seed crops for waste and later arrive at the barn for threshing. The history of birdseed and mixtures of birdseed is seemingly without end, and every author seems to possess the magic mix of seed. The basics are still to use black oil sunflower seed and the other sunflower types. From there, you can add almost anything in commercial seed and learn from firsthand experience what seed works the best in your region. I daresay that every select seed mix was derived exactly that way, and there are many select seed mixes out there that may not work well under your conditions. In other words, if one author tells you to put out cracked corn to attract a Lapland longspur, or that peanut butter will attract a rusty song sparrow or a varied thrush, don't hold your breath. A good selection and patience will work out best. Perusing the claims on seedbags is a great help. There are many transient birds on the wing, so offer a reasonable variety.

Commercial birdseed comes from a variety of companies, so you should be familiar with the type of seed itself and the various combinations.

One study by the U.S. Fish and Wildlife Service showed that black oil sunflower seed and white millet in separate feeders worked well. Most of the literature tables and charts indicate black oil sunflower seed as the favorite of most birds. However, recent experiments have shown that milo and millet were also well liked. There are still a variety of birds out there, and a good number of seeds in variety that specific birds enjoy. You could save your money and keep it simple, but it might not be as fascinating that way. Keep four or five small feeders and use them to experiment; it might contradict the experts.

Sunflower seed is available in five forms. Black oil sunflower seed, gray striped, black striped, hulled, and finch choice, which is a processed product. The preference for black oil sunflower seeds is in a high-seed-to-shell ratio and a high-oil content. Of all the sunflower seed varieties, the majority prefer black oil. Sunflower seeds are thin-shelled, easy to open, and rich in oil and protein. Virtually every bird likes them. In the winter, it might be worthwhile to supply hulled sunflower seeds as they're pure food and don't require as much time and energy to crack open in midwinter. In very cold weather, this could be a survival factor for some species where every calorie counts.

Because winter is the most important time for bird feeding, shelled peanuts are very rich in oil and protein and provide energy for high metabolism to help birds survive the many frigid nights of winter. The extra cost is negligible.

White proso millet is a favorite food of ground-feeders such as towhees, painted buntings, juncos, doves, cardinals, and purple finches. It contains starch, protein, and fats. Of all the small seeds, this is the preferred food. Thistle seed is like a magnet to a goldfinch; and it also attracts siskins and red polls, even if you've never had them. It is an excellent source of protein and fat for these birds.

There are many species of migratory and nonmigratory birds that breed in North America. Depending on where you are on the continent they may be known as songbirds, garden birds, or wild birds.

All of us have a farm supply store, pet store, hardware store, or garden center that has a good supply of the following seeds on hand. Read the information on the bag; it can help you decide which kinds of birds you want to attract to your yard.

Black oil sunflower seed—All seedeaters
Hulled sunflower seed—All seedeaters
Striped sunflower seed—titmouse, cardinal, blue jay, grosbeak, nuthatch
White millet seed—cardinal, towhee, junco, native, sparrow, chipping sparrow

Safflower seed—house finch, titmouse, cardinal, dove
Nutmeats—blue jay, woodpecker, titmouse
Pecans, filberts, almonds, walnuts—chickadee, nuthatch
Peanut pieces—titmouse, blue jay, chickadee, goldfinch, junco, woodpecker
Thistle seed—goldfinch, house finch, red poll, chickadee, pine siskin, dark-eyed junco
Fruit—oriole, mockingbird, woodpecker, starling, blue jay, thrush, bluebird, cardinal
Suet—woodpecker, chickadee, wren, nuthatch, cardinal, bluebird, blue jay, gold finch

Safflower is increasingly popular for cardinals, rose-breasted grosbeaks, chickadees, nuthatches, and mourning doves.

Milo (sorghum) is eaten by red-winged blackbirds, bobwhites, blue jays, dark-eyed juncos, chipping sparrows, and wood ducks.

Cracked corn is taken by indigo buntings, purple finches, rock doves, rose-breasted grosbeaks, goldfinches, blue jays, wood ducks, and mourning doves.

Niger thistle is a popular wildbird food and very attractive to American goldfinches, purple finches, song sparrows, red polls, mourning doves, red crossbills, and indigo buntings.

Canary seed is not a component of seed mixes.

White, golden, and red proso millet mixes are inexpensive and attract northern cardinals, mourning doves, purple finches, dark-eyed juncos, chipping sparrows, and song sparrows.

Peanut pickouts is a mixture of peanuts, pistachio nuts, pecans, cashews, and other nuts. Add to black oil sunflower seed at 10 percent and you'll have many cardinals.

Try all of these seeds and discover for yourself which ones work in your area. Preferences for food seem to vary. Older lists of seed preferences are a bit misleading and should not be taken literally.

Give authorities latitude. Results with the same seed vary with the region as birds forage a region for its native seed with instinctive skill. Black oil sunflower seeds should be the staple of all feeders. Ornithologists simply tell people to put out only black oil sunflower seeds as it meets the nutritional needs of almost all seedeaters. As per the Cornell experiments, the black-capped chickadee made visits 93 percent of the time to a sunflower seed feeder as opposed to 4 percent for millet and 3 percent for milo. The purple finch visited 77 percent sunflower seed feeders and the blue jay 73 percent. This about covers the overwhelming preference for sunflower seed—although milo and millet are still important. However, even birds deserve a buffet table of all the seeds listed, as well as finely diced table scraps.

Scraps

Birdseed will never be replaced, but interest in table scraps as provisions for the feeder is old and comes from experienced sources who faithfully dice all their leftovers for the birds and claim success. The following is only a short list of table scraps from many unknown sources. The list is endless; and remember, it's only a supplement to the seed:

Ground and dried meat
Finely broken eggshell
Grit
Fine sand
Oranges
Apples
Bananas
Bread and old crusts of bread
Cake
Coffee cake
Biscuits
Raisins

Oatmeal
Cottage cheese
Pecan meats
Cheese
Fresh tomatoes
Ham
Steak
Pork
Fried potatoes
Cantaloupe seed
Pie crust
Cookies
Watermelons

Various jellies and all baked goods (bread, rolls, coffee cake), left-over spaghetti or pasta (Roger Tory Peterson recommended this at a birding symposium that I attended.)

Be patient! Experiment, and try and try again.

These have all been verified as acceptable from experienced people with bird feeders. Obviously, birds in feeders will probably eat anything that qualifies as food for humans. This is even truer in the winter months and during emergency conditions. Again, a barn feeder keeps seed dry and palatable longer than any other feeder. The key is dicing the scraps as finely as possible. Also, suet, which is discussed in detail below, is essential for winter energy. Remember how difficult birds have it with a foot of snow on the ground.

Practically speaking, the above information is about all you need to know to begin feeding birds at your backyard feeding stations. Everyone uses his or her own experience. Birds have a seed preference, and if you have a preferred bird you would like to attract to your yard, it is worthwhile to put out their preference. (Keep in mind that black oil sunflower seed and hulled sunflower seed attracts all seedeaters throughout the year.)

Suet and Peanut Butter

In winter, suet is a treat for many birds. It is used as a supplement to increase numbers and types of birds that come to feeding stations. Because they have a seed preference, if you have a favorite bird you would like to attract to your yard, it is worthwhile to put out what they like.

Since suet is a high-calorie, energy-rich food for over eighty species of songbirds in North America, it is an essential ingredient in a balanced diet. Most often, suet—which is beef fat that forms around the kidney and liver—is available as raw fat in supermarkets and in a large variety of rendered forms with various amendments to make it more palatable to birds.

Of the species that eat suet, the energy they derive from it enables them to survive many a cold winter night. Their body temperature is 108 degrees Fahrenheit, and suet helps to maintain that level. Birds that eat suet include chickadees, titmice, nuthatches, downy woodpeckers, red-headed woodpeckers, flickers, and hairy woodpeckers. The consistent way to have a lot of woodpeckers and chickadees around your feeder is to have a suet feeder. They love suet and you may even be lucky enough to get a pileated woodpecker. Others might also include catbirds, wrens, and mockingbirds. Suet feeders are among the lowest priced of all birding apparatus. Plastic-coated wire baskets are available and will last for years. They are easily attached to a barn feeder, a post, or a tree, or even on a window frame.

The winter season is difficult for birds, to say the least. Food like suet provides heat and energy that is in short supply due to a lack of food from snow covering. Suet is not only a winter supplement. It is also a good "all-season" food that many species will eat the year-round, although the demand will be less in summer.

Remember, on cold winter days, it is instant energy. Obviously, they find it to be delicious. Suet can also be put out on a suet log, or on a stick hung on a limb or under a feeder, or on a post. It can also be placed in an old onion bag or smeared on rough bark. Simply look around your yard for a likely spot for its location. I don't know what percentage of a bird's diet comes from a feeder, but where in the wild can a bird benefit from any one supplement more than suet?

Peanut butter is also a good source of energy and protein. There are no cases of birds choking on peanut butter. Both ingredients yield the high-energy content required by wild songbirds. Rendered suet and peanut butter can also be put out in drilled logs or pieces of wood. In addition to oil and protein, peanut butter seems to contain all the salt that birds need and, for those that eat it, provides the energy to survive the freezing days of winter, especially if you add cornmeal to it. In fact, many consider peanut butter to be an essential ingredient in their feeding programs. Birds not only love it, but it's an inexpensive meal that offers them high protein and energy. As their protein intake is low during the winter, peanut butter is an excellent way to provide a nutritional supplement at this critical time of the year.

Keep in mind the great energy requirements of birds in winter, when natural sources are at a yearly low. Look at the strain put on the acidic soils and shaded forests to yield berries and fruit that formerly helped to supply similar levels of energy, as those provided by suet.

Some eighty species of wild birds are attracted to and eat suet. Additionally, suet and meat scraps are standard food items for insectivorous birds, as they act as incentives to draw other than the usual species that you normally see in your yard. Suet and peanut butter provide a balanced diet when insects are scarce. Although less conspicuous, when birds eat suet, they are really after carrion (homemade suet, commercial suet, or beef fat supplies have the same nutrients).

Bluebird lovers are often rewarded with mealworms, which also attract gray catbirds, cardinals, woodpeckers, chickadees, titmice, nuthatches, wrens, mockingbirds, and many others. Place the worms on a platform so the birds can see them move and wiggle.

(Hummingbirds do not eat seed; they drink sweetened water. Therefore, you should consider a hummingbird feeder that can fit in the area provided for your feeder or feeding station.) Add grit to your feeder in the winter and spring. Birds have no teeth with which to grind their food; they use the grit and sand in their crops, which helps them grind their food. Crushed eggshells do the same thing.

There is considerable advice available about backyard birding that will add to your understanding of the written and unwritten rules. Many books are available at libraries and bookstores. Seed companies and stores selling seed have literature as well. The Department of the Interior in Washington, D.C., and the Audubon Society in your local area also have books available. A typical bird library in America is filled with many volumes. The wisest thing to do is begin searching these sources on your own. It's a labor of love that will bring rich rewards.

Birdbaths

Birdbaths are definitely an added attraction to the feeding and housing complex. Usually, garden supply stores have a good variety on hand, including the traditional concrete pedestal and basin. In recent years, some basins that sit on the ground add a touch of nature. Plumbing fixtures that keep the water full and circulating and even warm in the wintertime are now available. Obviously, birders are very creative people who can find many ways of putting water to work for them.

The question of birdbath placement has to be considered. Usually, a bush, shrub, or tree should be nearby, so that a bird can take shelter in case of a predator.

Birds take dust baths in sand, snow baths in the snow, and water baths in warm sunshine. English sparrows and robins are usually the greatest bathers of all (although, this past summer, we have had catbirds, and a pair of mourning doves frequents our birdbath every morning and evening).

Why do birds bathe and preen? I believe that they know it's good for them.

Place a water bath near feeders for the birds' convenience and for viewing them from the inside. The usual depth of the water would be two to three inches. The birds will get used to it. There is not much more to say about birdbaths. The garden centers have all the supplies required. You're on your own in this area. My preference is a bath on a pedestal. I've seen and admired many baths cut from stone and faced with flagstone. Use your imagination! Visit a garden center.

CHAPTER 4

Birdhouses

When I was a young man in Fairfield, Connecticut, I was eagerly learning the business of landscape design. One day, at a well-landscaped home, I noticed a clay agricultural drain tile fastened under the eaves. Grass and twigs were sticking out of the end, and the beaks of the baby birds could be seen protruding above the rim of the nest. This was my first encounter with the divine charm of having birds in a garden. This beautiful moment has never left my memory. The startling simplicity of a bird habitat, in the form of a foot-long drainage tile, added something special—even if the tile's original purpose was much different.

About twelve years ago, I noticed that clay flowerpots were something that could be converted into a bird habitat with a little fashioning. With some trial and error, I was able to create bird-nesting cavities in three sizes out of these clay flowerpots. For the first three years, purple finches occupied them, and then, when the finch population declined, the titmice and chickadees found them useful. These flowerpot houses not only made good nesting

View of clay pot houses and feeders hanging in our barn

sites, but they also served as excellent seed dispensers for all bird species. They held a good amount and kept them dry—and small birds loved them!

One day, the town clerk asked me to make a bluebird house. I looked up the specifications and constructed a house that was five by five on the inside floor, eight inches from the bottom of the entrance hole to the bottom of the cavity, and topped with a pitched roof. I was able to put it together easily and, by extension, it seemed reasonable to speculate that possibilities in design with wood were endless. The appropriate design could meet the needs of the many wild songbirds that have a most difficult time in finding a natural cavity in a tree, a stump, or a fence post. As mankind has recklessly changed the forests in America to meet the needs of development, the trees with cavities have fallen to the bucksaw and chainsaw. We are just beginning to see the damage wrought for the sake of profit under the guise of "jobs" and strengthening the economy. The first principle of God is husbandry; the affairs of man always follow this. Folks who mount bird-nesting boxes along trails or around the house will be part of the new husbandry.

The great success of the bluebird house along countless miles of trails is the greatest testament of this attention to nature. In the past, the USDA has set up cavity boxes in the vicinity of certain crops and introduced birds that would eat the insects harming the crops. The successful results galvanize the reputation of the birdhouse.

One of the best things about birdhouses is the wonderful experience of seeing the birds take advantage of their new shelter. I saw a pair of bluebirds use a birdhouse I had just mounted on a pipe and put into a field at eight that morning. I have one customer who told me that a bird was in the house the same day he put it up. Birdhouses work! Don't hesitate to put up five to six houses, even on a small piece of property. Pitched-roof houses can be hung from eaves and porches, or placed on a pipe or fence post or into a tree. Rest assured, birds will accept them and move in.

Remember that wood birdhouses will be warmer in winter and cooler in summer. The types of wood that are generally used are cedar, white pine, and poplar. If you have a special wood, you can use it, but just make sure that it isn't unseasoned wood, which has a tendency to warp, crack, and split. I have used black walnut for feeders, and it's exquisite. I recommend that the reader consider using lumber from the mill of 3/4-inch thickness for feeders and nesting boxes. Use two-inch galvanized deck screws (preferably with a square head, but a Phillips will do just as well) and an electric screwdriver. Avoid using nails unless it is absolutely necessary, and then only the galvanized kind. Drastic changes in temperature tend to loosen and weaken a nailed-together birdhouse. The square-head screws can help by providing 25 percent more torque and a tight-fitting structure. This prevents the loosening of houses by expansion from cold. The tighter the structure, the longer it will last.

The finish on a birdhouse or feeder can be a matter of taste and decor. Most people want a natural, rustic look. Still, it is a good idea to apply three to four coats of polyurethane to the roof of either structure to make it totally impervious to water. The better the protection, the longer the structure will last. Copper or galvanized sheet metal also makes an ideal roof.

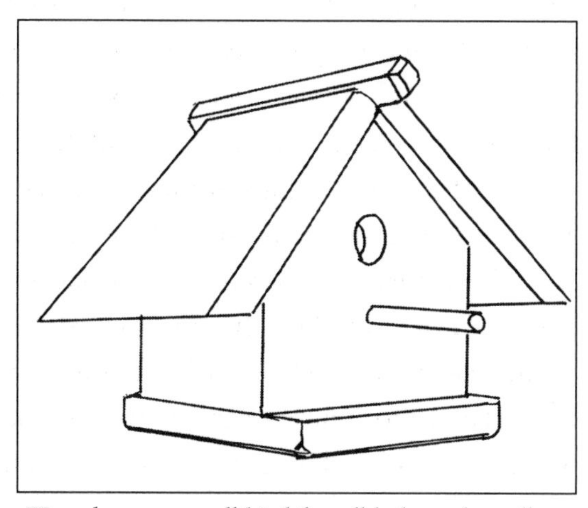

Wren house—small bird (small hole and small house)

It is interesting to note that it is not the outside structure of the birdhouse that attracts the birds but the hole or cavity in the structure. From a distance, this black hole is very conspicuous, especially in the spring. They will be attracted to the black hole in the house, which is similar to the cavity in a tree. Birdhouses can be put up at any time of the year and should remain up the entire year. Birds explore birdhouses all year.

In the spring, there is nesting; and in the winter, birdhouses offer protection from the cold, even though the nests are still intact. Three people have told me they saw a birdhouse, on a frigid winter morning, housing five to six birds. (This, of course, leads to the roosting box or over winter house, in several designs, that could hold ten to fifteen birds on perches, which is ideal for the backyard birder.)

If you make your own birdhouse, you can follow the dimensions on the chart provided on page 87 and create your own design. You might even try some barn siding and experiment with this unique wood.

How many should you put up? Birds of different species live well with one another. For two years, I mounted flowerpot houses on a telephone pole about five feet away from a busy highway. Finches have nested twice in these pots about twenty feet from nesting robins and seventy-five feet from wrens. As a rule of thumb, I tell people to keep up six houses. On ten acres, I would imagine that fifty nest boxes would be of great help. Space at random distances of 150 to 200 feet on center. The homeowner with ten nesting boxes skillfully placed will be rewarded with deeper pleasure than one with just two. I have actually heard of homes of several acres with three hundred birdhouses. Putting up birdhouses might be a bit tricky because birds are definitely territorial, and anything closer than fifty feet might not be tolerable. On the other hand, we have heard, from many people, of communal associations that seem to defy territoriality. Territoriality also applies to birds of the same species because competition for similar food becomes critical. Supplemental feeding, however, crosses boundaries.

There is the question of certain-sized holes for certain birds. I'm not sure that works as well as it might. Do birds consider the size of the hole or the lines of the interior? I think they look more at the interior and don't think much about the exterior. The chart on page 87 will give the appropriate-sized hole, depending on the birds you are trying to attract. The standard 1½-inch is used on our cavity nesters.

Mounting the birdhouses is easy. The flat-backed bluebird house can be mounted on a pole or fence post, or on the house. Often they are fastened to a pipe with a "C" clamp. Check with a hardware store for flange and pipe. Birdhouses are mounted on a pipe by first screwing a cast-iron flange on the bottom of the house. Use a seven-foot pipe, two feet in the ground, on which to mount the house. Then screw the house on the threaded pipe. Pitched-roof birdhouses can also be hung by screwing an eye into the middle of the peak of the roof. Another eye screw is then mounted under a branch or an eave and the two connected with an "S" hook. Of course, there are variations on all of this. The nesting box placed at five feet above the ground provides the ideal substitute for natural cavities in trees and fence posts that are no longer in place.

Above all, design your own house. I constructed five houses from plans and I didn't like any of them. I learned that originality works best.

A home bird garden is not a wilderness, but with selected wild plants in variety and composition it is an improvement on the wilderness. Birdhouses appropriately spaced in a bird garden provide a wilderness in microcosm . . . husbanded and intense . . . a nesting haven . . . a place of protection. It can be taken on faith that nesting boxes and birdhouses of sound construction will be found and used by birds.

With wrens, it is possible to have one house in the front yard and one in the backyard. Birdhouses are available that hang flat against a wall and, thus, at eight feet or so, are free from squirrels and cats.

Other designs with pitched roofs can be hung from branches, porches, and eaves. They are also a good addition.

The history of ornithology in America is replete with examples of scientists and bird-watchers who have mounted hundreds of thousands of nesting boxes for the cavity-nesting species with excellent results. In most cases, they had definite purposes and species in mind. While the birds seem to adapt to man-made nesting boxes, this does not mean they will give up nesting in natural cavities. Their preference? Who knows. Once nesting boxes are put out on trees, posts, pipes, and on houses and barns, the number that will be occupied will reveal the acute shortage of natural cavities. Natural cavities are rare. Where can they nest? Certainly not in new-growth forests.

Success in building bird populations is dependent upon the homeowner in mounting a generous number of nesting boxes. Birds will occupy about half of them in a given year. Nestlings can be looked at in several ways. Birdhouses are constructed with swinging and sliding doors. The best policy is taking a short peek! Don't bother them too much. Like the farmers say, "Leave birds alone!"

Slate roof with steel duck (cut out) placed on birdhouse roof

Be realistic. Wood is wood is wood, and it needs help and, like any house, it needs maintenance. I make it a point to chat with a regional antique dealer who deals with many antique birdhouses, which would never have survived their fifty years or more without a few coats of paint. I remember many small birdhouses built years ago that were well coated with white paint that preserved the house. I also have seen birdhouses put out and showing rot in only five years. Obviously, they were never treated well. Polyurethane or preservatives applied to the roof would have extended their life. A weathered birdhouse is a fine idea, but the life of the house will be cut short just as the interior is getting cozy and more like a home for the birds. Preservation and conservation applies to essential functions like houses and feeders.

Of all the cavity-nesting birds, the wren is the easiest to attract to your yard using one or two houses. A wren may have two wives, and this means a lot of singing. Wrens are constant entertainment and perky, to say the least. Often a Bewicks wren, with a more charming voice/song than the house wren, will arrive; and you will be fascinated no end. They will come and depart on schedule if they have a house. The point here, as with all cavity-nesting birds, is to always have the houses ready, and the birds will arrive with a song.

I have had a lot of experience with the public in this area, and I know that many birdhouses wind up in the garage and never see the light of day! For the bird, it's a question of "availability." Make the nesting box "available" about March first or so and it will be inspected, even if you don't see them doing this. Add the word *access* to your bird vocabulary and you have the entrance hole in mind. Winter temperatures of zero to ten degrees below zero are bitter, and many birds that have not been feeding may not survive. It has long been known that birds occupy birdhouses all winter to escape the cold. One lady reported that twenty wrens entered a large birdhouse, but she didn't see them leave. On another occasion, ten bluebirds entered a flicker house that was seven by seven by eighteen inches tall. Even birds that build open nests will come into a cavity to escape the cold.

Bear in mind that with a foot of snow on the ground that covers normal access to any food, the significance of the birdhouse to survival is apparent. With this in mind, the development of the winter roosting box seems natural. The best roosting boxes are from two to three feet tall and ten to eighteen inches wide on the inside. At the bottom is a one and a $1^1/_2$-inch or larger hole. Inside are perches that may hold ten, twenty, or perhaps thirty birds. If made of one-inch white pine, it will be well insulated. I don't know what the shortfall is in nesting boxes in Connecticut, but a liberal estimate would be a half-million. Birds are intuitive animals. This means that they have been programmed to expect cavities to be readily available at nesting time. Without a natural cavity or birdhouse, they can't succeed. With no public understanding or grasp of the plight of cavity-nesting birds, the mistakes of the past will be repeated.

One of the most common reasons given for not putting up birdhouses is that people never see any birds. I remind them that if they put up the birdhouses, the birds will be there. Even then, they aren't sure! Some people reported success in luring birds by putting some seed in the hole of the house. This sounds like an interesting idea, but not necessary. In this regard, when I sell at craft shows, countless people ask if they should put seed in the hole of a birdhouse, thinking it can serve as a feeder. Conversely, they call a feeder a birdhouse. This has made me wonder!

Birds have excellent sight and can spot a black hole from a considerable distance. At a recent outdoor craft show, I left my display of birdhouses and feeders uncovered for the night. Upon arriving early the next morning for the show, there were five to six birds on the display. Exhibitors that had arrived earlier said that the birds were already in the houses. Now, this was in the middle of a football field and there was a wooded area about five hundred feet away. Obviously, the structure of a birdhouse is as meaningless to a bird as a dead tree, but they did see the black holes almost immediately! If you think about it, the first thing we look for when approaching a house is the front door. Obviously, what a bird looks for on a birdhouse is the black hole (*its* front door).

Don't think of how many birdhouses you want to put up, but how many black holes to present for their inspection. Think the way a bird thinks. If you do, you will have many birds flocking to your garden. When you put up a feeder, you are truly thinking like a bird, which is about food! When you provide for them, they will come.

Housing and feeding are the heart of a sanctuary, and the presence of birds on the wing is the reward. The birds build afresh each spring. It is a part of the breeding process and, depending on the bird, is an instinctive task. Without a number of nesting boxes, spring would not be the same. This is the time of year when territoriality is proclaimed and the birdhouse is the center of it all. The birdhouse is for courting and nest building and another life cycle. It is the most active and busiest at this time of the year, and we can be interested witnesses.

I'm not sure what makes a bird choose a specific house, but it has something to do with the interior, time, and weathering. However, I have had many people tell me that my new houses had takers immediately. Wood from the mill is rough cut and sometimes weathered and, at a one-inch thickness, it may be appealing because of soundness. A ledge or platform with a roof will attract robins and phoebes without fail.

Communal living seems acceptable to many birds under specific conditions. Communal housing is available with up to four or more cavities and is used regularly. Many people seem to be bothered that snakes, mice, raccoons, and other birds will get into their birdhouses if they put them up. This fear is exaggerated and can be allayed by putting up a few more houses. In any case, this is also the natural relation between creatures who are not killers, but merely looking for food.

One of the best ways to stop predators when the house is on a pipe is to mount a squirrel baffle (some people do not like the look of a baffle, but it does the job), or take your chances. An eighteen-inch length of white PVC pipe around a wooden post is very effective in that animals can't grip it. A generous amount of axle grease is good, also. See a tinsmith and have a copper baffle handcrafted; this inverted cone stops squirrels.

Birdhouses should be cleaned before March first. That is when migrating birds return. With the chickadee, titmouse, downy woodpecker, and nuthatch, place wood chips in the house up to the hole. This is a strong attraction for these species. On the other hand, many old farmers contradict this and maintain that the birds always clean out the boxes and point out a birdhouse that has had birds for ten years with no cleaning by the farmer!

Of some interest is providing birds with nesting materials. They readily use cotton, string, thread, unraveled rope, moss, fur, and cloth strips. Commercial material is also available. Cut four-inch lengths. Scatter on the lawn or driveway. Of course, dried grass, weeds, lawn cuttings, and so on are always welcome. Birds are naturally capable of finding their own natural materials.

There is a problem with starlings and English sparrows occupying the nesting boxes of native songbirds. The Department of the Interior has taken these birds from legal protection. The advice is to dump their nests. The decision to remove them from the protected list was welcomed. The starlings and sparrows are undesirable in that they chase the wild songbirds away.

A number of people have remarked that, even over a number of years, their birdhouse is not occupied. I tell them to move it to a different spot and also put up more houses. Face the access hole to an open area.

Cleaning a birdhouse should be an interesting event when you recognize the importance of sanitation. Like other animals, birds have an assortment of mites and lice and other pests. I have heard it recommended that birds arriving in the spring would clean nesting boxes. It sounds reasonable, but cleaning it yourself might be best. Taking houses down for the winter and cleaning and repairing them is a good discipline. Some authors claim that a sealed box is worthless after two nestings. Others deny this.

Cleaning the box is good husbandry.

Squirrels are in the habit of making the holes of a birdhouse larger. A good solution is to measure the size of the hole and purchase a circular drill of that diameter. Secure some sheet copper and on a six-inch-square sheet, cut a hole in the middle. Fit the cut copper over the hole and fasten with suitable brads—it can be trimmed as a round or left as a square of an appropriate size. Also, try a washer, if you can find one that's the right size. Drill and mount with screws or brads. Copper is very ornamental and with sharp shears, you can do a fancy job.

Birdhouse with copper ring around the hole

One of the purposes of the birds is to keep the insect population down but not eliminate it. There is a spiritual aspect to this function that we can't escape. God made some birds to eat the insects and keep them under control but not eliminate them.

I believe the wild songbird is an expression of the spirit, and we are expressly responsible to God to husband the birds until a permanent culture on the land arrives to do the work. As for the birds, they are in dire need of a permanent ecology. The birdhouse or nesting box is a requirement for their continued survival. You should make them to fit the rural milieu using rough wood and barn siding that's plain and not garish—something to complement the countryside. Put up strong houses and secure them with drywall screws.

Just put the boxes up.
All nature seems at work.
Slugs leave their lair, the bees are
Stirring, birds are on the wing.

—Samuel Taylor Coleridge

In the spring, among songbirds, the cavity in a tree provides temporary quarters for the purpose of breeding in season. They range from a pouch assembled of sticks to the intricate formed cup of straw and grass. Each species seems to be in instinctual possession of the pattern for faithful repeats in nest construction. The selection of a cavity that offers protection seems to be another constant. The construction of a nest starts with larger twigs that decrease in size until straw and grass are added to created the cozy environment for eggs and nestlings. Subsequent nesting may include cleaning out the entire nest or adjusting in small ways and revising.

The cavity-nesting birds are those species that, if nature were left untouched, would find a cavity in a tree made by a woodpecker. Given the constantly changing landscape of the United States, the oldest forests don't provide enough aged trees with dead wood for cavities. We have shaped the land and surroundings to meet the requirements of transient economic trending. How is it possible for the natural economy of the area to provide trees of age and mature wood for cavities? It doesn't seem like it will unless our economies adapt to natural systems. We act like we are not on this planet for the long haul. Natural systems will not survive the human abstract of money because our yield off the land far exceeds what we put back into it.

Something like fifty years ago every farm in the East had at least one nesting pair of bluebirds. Clearly, bluebird populations are far down from what they should be, and it is safe to assume that populations of other cavity-nesters are down as a result of the change from an agricultural economy and the way farmers shaped the land for

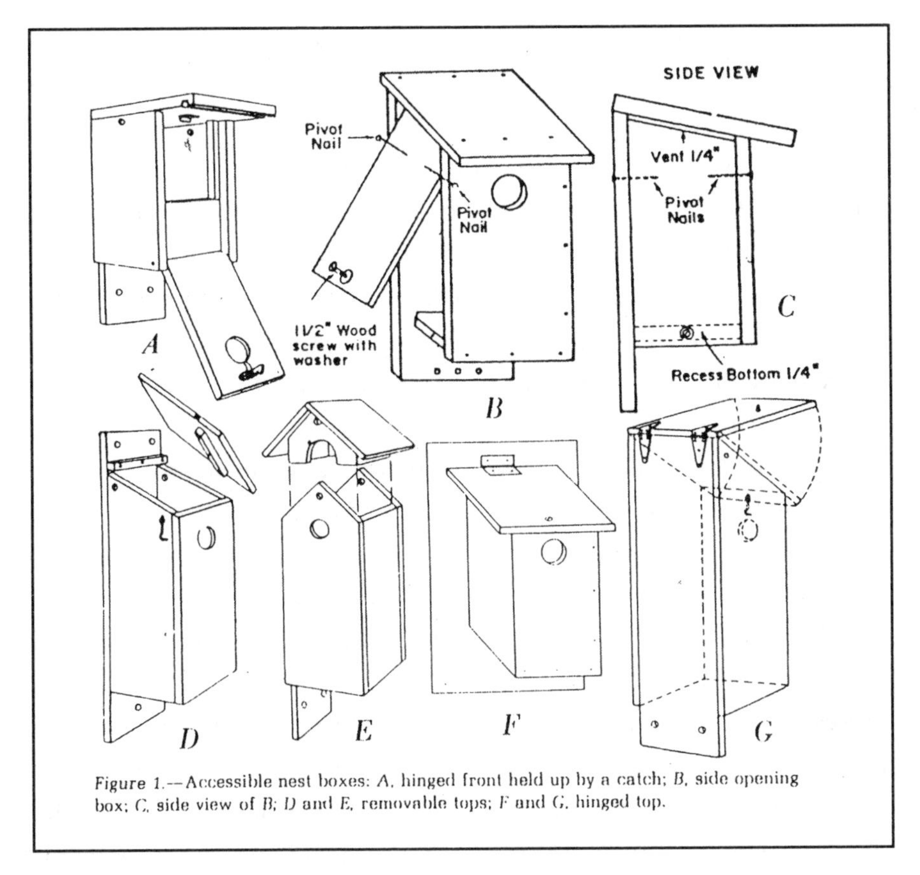

Figure 1.--Accessible nest boxes: *A*, hinged front held up by a catch; *B*, side opening box; *C*, side view of *B*; *D* and *E*, removable tops; *F* and *G*, hinged top.

USDA Bulletin

long-term interests. *This allowed for the retention of larger and even ideal specimen trees.*

Property owners should be actively interested in mounting six to twelve homemade or purchased nesting boxes with the hope of having bird families in half the houses every year. Most species may nest two to three times a year.

As a builder of birdhouses and feeders, I mounted ten around our house. I personally know they work well, and many of my customers tell me about their success. One time I lifted the roof on a wall-hanging birdhouse and a female chickadee instantly covered the eggs with one wing. Needless to say, the top went back fast.

As to availability of nesting cavities, most Americans would have a difficult time imagining the state of a virgin forest as an ideal for all birds. In areas of human habitation, trees of age do not abound. The proven and practical thing to do is to mount the nesting box or the birdhouse. Birdhouses should be considered as essential to the birds. Pretty much that simple. When the original soils become depleted, we add minerals. Add nesting boxes as well. What was original must be duplicated . . . as in a rural milieu. Older volumes on birdhouses show sound structures permanently nailed together. When the structures rotted or came apart, they were replaced but never cleaned out. It may or may not be presumptuous to think we have to clean out houses for the birds. They have no problem cleaning natural cavities that are moist with rotting wood. They never needed any person to clean out a cavity in any tree for tens of thousands of years. It is curious that we deprive them of their natural habitat and range and then insist on the artifice of trapdoors, sliding doors, steel and brass hinges, and hooks. Maybe, the simpler the better. Man has yet to understand gardens, landscapes, nature, or any sense of husbandry in our own suburban home on the range. The birdhouse is not natural, but the cavity is. Make it unobtrusive. That is, keep it simple. The house is not natural. The cavity is. But this is not time to split hairs. At any number of craft shows, people have asked me, "Why is that hole in that box?" In effect, some people don't know much about birdhouses.

Birdhouses are inexpensive and can be easily made at home.

It is claimed that birding is second only to gardening in popularity. The bird ecology will improve as the landscape psyche improves in the United States. People serious about landscape will put out birdhouses in new and old gardens. So, create a new garden, a new landscape, and a new habitat for your birds. You will be doing yourself and your planet a favor.

Roosting Houses

Roosting box

The roosting house is made for the purpose of giving birds shelter from the winter cold. Roosting houses vary in size, from one that holds up to ten birds and ten perches to twenty birds and twenty perches. I have made many roosting boxes, or as I call them, "overwintering houses." Mine are all custom designed and are eighteen to twenty-four inches long with a sloped roof, and are twelve inches wide. They have ten perches and a 1½-inch entry hole and perch just outside of it. For aesthetics, the roof and front are made of various barn sidings. They can be mounted on a pole or, my preference, put up on a wall.

There is a long history of open- and cavity-nesting birds occupying available birdhouses to capacity during zero degree weather. While selling birdhouses at craft shows, I have met people who claim to have witnessed birdhouses filling up with birds during the early hours of the evening. These people also witnessed them emptying out in the morning. One lady testified that twenty wrens arrived intermittently and entered a large birdhouse before dark. Another person said eight different species departed from a roosting box in the early morning hours. Another couple saw seven birds leave a birdhouse around seven in the morning. About twenty people have related similar stories to me about the popularity of these roosting houses.

I am told by ornithologists that this has been observed for many years and that a variety and multiplicity of birds do congregate in roosting houses and even birdhouses to escape the frigid cold. Differences in bird variety don't matter as much when birds are cold. Even the open nesters forget disparity. Practicality wins out in the end, and intense cold creates a brotherhood of body heat.

In the Northeast especially, winter can be a devastating time for birds. With temperatures of ten degrees Fahrenheit and lower, this is when the roosting box and the birdhouse serve the purpose of saving birds from freezing to death in these low temperatures. Also, if there is a covering of snow, then food becomes scarcer.

When my wife and I drive to craft shows, she monitors the grounds of homes and assures me that birdhouses are not common; and we wonder how wild songbirds make it without a warm house or cavity for shelter in the winter.

A winter roosting house is a good addition to any property. That roosting boxes have been around for many years with success and yet are not in use among avid backyard birders, or are mostly unheard of, is a curiosity. Certainly, most people who have birdhouses are not aware of their dual function, but should be. Houses should be cleaned in the fall and then put up in anticipation of a cold winter. Do not take houses down for the winter. Leave them up for the birds. With birdhouses cleaned for the winter, a roosting box, a water supply, and feeding station, you have created a small sanctuary! Even an uncleaned birdhouse will be very cozy for one or two birds. A good functioning feeding station would certainly include a place for a roosting box. It adds to the meaning of sanctuary.

The design can be your own but there are some general guidelines. Entrance holes may be 1½-inches to 2½-inches to allow easy entrance. A perch or flat platform is also helpful. I have made roosting houses in different sizes. An average height would be two feet tall with the inside dimensions in the range of eight by twelve inches and up to sixteen total perches mounted on both sides.

Think of how large a natural cavity may be and how many birds that may hold.

Roosting boxes can save many birds on cold winter nights.

Remember the significance of the cavity to the bird. The cavity access hole attracts the birds. Because it means shelter on a cold night, it looks the same on a tree trunk or a roosting box.

Simple roosting box

Again, the black hole is significant to the bird from a considerable distance. With roosting boxes, many black holes provide a multiple offering of shelter. Seeing a black hole in the distance is a blessing for a bird in a storm.

Construction of roosting houses can be made more efficient and hold more heat if made of white pine 3/4 to one inch in thickness for insulation. Sealing the joints would also be helpful.

Placing them on the south side of a house or barn would increase the opportunity to build up some solar heat. Also, a dark wood stain might help enhance the absorption of heat.

Birds that might have sought shelter in thick evergreen shrubbery would be happy to find a roosting box and, with eight ot ten other birds in occupancy, the temperature would go up. Birdhouses and roosting boxes offer big advantages to the backyard birder in not only attracting a population of birds but also preserving and protecting them.

Open front on hinge

Cleaning Houses

Many people have talked to me on the subject of whether birdhouses should be cleaned once a year or left for the next occupant to clean. In the last forty years or so, many birdhouse manufacturers have provided mechanisms for cleaning birdhouses by using a system of hinges, latches, hooks, and sliding doors that works well. The problem is that these parts begin to loosen due to constant freezing and thawing. I have witnessed these nails being almost phased out because of the problem of them coming loose.

On trips to Indiana for the past ten years, my wife and I traveled many miles along fencing that had birdhouses on posts every three hundred feet or so. These were nesting boxes with four by four inside and a 1$^1/_2$-inch hole. Every box was securely nailed together with no latches, no hooks, and no hinges. The more experienced I become, the more obvious it seems that the birdhouses for the past two hundred years were probably simple boxes nailed together. When they decayed, they were just replaced rather than repaired. In the spring, the nesting birds selected an access hole and began emptying the contents. This probably didn't take too long and if the bird still liked the house, he would arrange his own nest.

In the northwestern part of Connecticut, I know four retired farmers who have put out many, many boxes for birds to nest in over the past fifty years or so. Each one insists that not *one* of them was ever cleaned. They maintain that the bird will clean out the house "every time"—this from men of the land. I'm sure other farmers do the same as these practical men. I've looked at many old birdhouses at an antique dealer's. He scouts a region in his car and when he sees one, he makes an offer. They are homemade, very interesting in color, original construction, weathered, and have seen many springs and summers. Only a few have sliding or hinged doors, most are nailed or screwed together, and some still have the nesting material inside. The literature from the early twentieth century (when birdhouses were put out by the USDA) depicts that birdhouses were simply nailed together and the newly arriving birds cleaned them out for their own nesting or left them intact.

To clean or not, that's the question! I think this will be proven by the ornithologists if they don't already know it or have not expressed it. The information I have from my farmer friends in northwestern Connecticut is probably true. When men on the land witness it and say you do not have to open a box at any time, it is based on sound observation of the same houses for a number of years. When the house is worn or decay sets in, a new house is put out and the observation continues. I notice many more birdhouses in garden and bird stores that are permanently nailed together. When they are screwed together, one side can be removed and the house cleaned. I think it will always be an option. The long-term view will be that of the farmer and practical people on the land.

Keep it simple. Use of soap and water and disinfectant might be for the overanxious. Cavities high up in dead trunks have served as homes for the birds for thousands of years. When the bird arrives at a cavity, he cleans it, and then lays in his own nesting materials. Some people have gone to the trouble of laying out string, thread, and rope to help the birds. There are even sources for thread and string (which might be commercializing nature . . . too much).

Cleaning birdhouses is a nice ritual and should be encouraged. It means you care about and love the birds. However, if you have a house that's high in a tree to attract a certain bird, it is easier and wiser to let the birds do all the cleaning. In nature, a bird does not look for a human being to clean out a house or actual cavity. I fasten my houses with square head two- to four-inch screws so the bottom can be removed for cleaning.

Birds are diligent workers. After watching wrens perform this chore, cleaning a nest box is hardly a task for any bird. Providing a clean box is still a good feeling. The old answer is: It depends. Setting out string, and cleaning and disinfecting hinges, latches, hooks, and special-sized holes for specific birds, is overdoing a good thing. Leaving them alone is sage, but rarely listened to, advice.

I think the time is approaching in America when people will be feeding and housing more birds for fun. They will be like the American husbandman, who loves the land and the green plants and knows the godly connection. Green plants are our actual connection to the birds. For the seed it eats, the bird is beholden to the green plant, as the plant is beholden to the bird for eating the insects that might decimate it.

The tubefeeder is a foolish distraction, an accidental invention that made a hit when something was needed to supply seeds to birds that needed food. It served a good purpose. As mentioned earlier, birdhouses and feeders should be thought of as garden art. This will have the effect of building an interest in the garden rather than the "yard." People jump from "yard" to "garden" quickly, once the difference occurs to them.

What happens with birds looking for a nesting site varies. They may clean out the box entirely; they may take out half the grass, or all of it. They surely will improvise and do exactly what suits their needs. We should think less about cleaning out, for the birds left alone will make the decision of how and when to clean. There is nothing to say a cleaned-out box has the greater appeal. As my farmer friends say, "Leave the birds alone!"

CHAPTER 5

Squirrels

Bird lovers unite! What can you do about squirrels? A number of things. And yet the squirrels seem brighter than people. A rustic barn feeder of barn siding that I designed and built has no effect on the disrespectful squirrels. They have no aesthetic sense. They are as indifferent to a good design as to a plastic feeding tube. Obviously, the seeds are their bag and, if I were a squirrel, I would do likewise.

I have sold barn feeders at craft shows for twelve years. It comes down to speaking to thousands of people about feeders, their experiences, and their fascinating squirrel problems. One man describes his experience as "the life and times of a squirrel smarter than me." This is the story of many, many people who have come to know this critter firsthand, and never failed to outwit them. Of course, it's all good natural banter that seems to indicate that man has more than met his match. (If a squirrel were elected president, the seedy Congress would be dispatched quickly.) Claims as to the wisdom of squirrels and their limitless patience are without end.

Eyewitnesses have reported squirrels that have leaped twelve feet horizontally and six feet straight up. Descriptions of how they dismantle plastic feeders are a testament to their genius. No animal has as intense a gaze and studies so intensely the task at hand: getting tasty sunflower seeds. The bird lover doesn't want the squirrel to have this food that is meant for the birds.

The word is *squirrel-proofing.* Many people prefer not to put out birdseed at all when the price exacted by pillaging squirrels is so high. These folks love the birds, but the cost of having the squirrel eat 75 percent of it decreases the incentive to put out seed. Under these circumstances, many birds suffer unnecessarily.

Bird feeders have been provided with a number of squirrel preventors: plastic and sheet metal baffles; greased poles; Ben-Gay on the pole; highly polished poles; telescopic poles; or feeders hung with monofilament, copper, or sheet metal roofs so squirrels can't jump on them. At the Cornell Lab of Ornithology, they are experimenting with a system of baffle placements.

Baffles have been made from garbage can lids and six-inch polyvinyl chloride pipes that are placed under a feeder (making it very difficult for the squirrel to hold on). Feeders hanging on a horizontal line can have lengths of plastic pipe around the wire, which turn and spin the line. Of course, there is the counterweighted sheet metal feeder, which many say is very good at deterring squirrels.

I have heard of small transformers that deliver a small jolt to squirrels. Individual imagination may be the final answer. The use of hot pepper recipes in the seed mix has been reported as being good by some and not so good by others.

Many people don't mind feeding squirrels at all. In fact, some people will place raw peanuts in the shell and crushed corn out for their furry-tailed friends. This is at least an expedient in outsmarting them. However, serious backyard bird feeders with ambitions for feeding station status will want better control over who feeds at their feeders.

Barn feeders are getting a great deal of attention because they hold large quantities of seed and, except in a heavy driving rain, keep it dry. Aesthetically, they have great appeal and are very rustic. If you place a copper squirrel-proof roof on it, the leaping squirrel hits the roof, has no hold, and falls to the ground. A squirrel-proof pole should be another important consideration when putting up a barn feeder. If you purchase a seven- to eight-foot pipe that holds the feeder about six feet from the ground, think only of how you can fashion the pipe so that the squirrel can't climb it. This opens the door for many deep thinkers.

Potential bird feeders do not have to be thwarted. There are a number of matters to consider for squirrel-proof feeders. The consideration must be for the birds and the pleasure of the provider of seed. Birds in our time require year-round supplemental feeding and if squirrels are depriving the birds of a necessity, a sort of bird husbandry must be put in place. Bird husbandry simply means highly preferential treatment of the birds.

Personally, I love squirrels, but the ecology of the birds is paramount because their natural ecology has long since departed. It might be a question of a separate ecology for the squirrels that belong as much as the birds, if that is your liking. Squirrels consume so much of the seed in feeders that the provider won't supply it, this is a tremendous loss to the birds. Hundreds of birders have told me this over the past twelve years. Their answers are various: It's discouraging or too expensive.

A squirrel cannot leap six to ten feet, land on a copper or sheet metal roof, and stay there. He will slide and land on the ground. Backyard birding can be the hobby in the United States if the squirrel factor can be changed in positive ways.

The next to the last resort is an animal trap, and those who have tried it have reported good results (many, many squirrels have been caught and transported far away to wooded areas). I show birdhouses and feeders at the Connecticut State Museum of Natural History every spring. The wife of a professor is an ardent birder with great squirrel problems. One year she trapped fifteen squirrels (Have A Heart Trap) and dropped them off in a forest preserve. Many people do this successfully. It seems to be a simple solution to a persistent problem.

Squirrels in a natural setting would get along well without sunflower seeds, milo, cracked corn, or millet that they find in feeders. Backyard birders, and a few people who operate feeding stations of some complexity with only the birds in mind may or may not want to feed the squirrels, or the bears, deer, or raccoons. The birds have exclusivity. Certainly squirrels, bears, deer, and raccoons are creatures of nature, but competing with birds for food in the backyard is a similar transgression to the wolves and mountain lions, which are the curse of the ranchers, and deer that damage crops.

The squirrel, of course, was always a miracle to me—as are all creatures, both furry and feathered. What is better than having a list of fifty bird species visiting your feeder in a year? Is it not better to bring the birds to you, where they can be seen only a few feet away, rather than go on a weekend pilgrimage to shore and forest to see them only at a considerable distance?

Birds and squirrels belong in nature, but in a noncompetitive way. Backyard bird feeding and squirrels don't mix. There must be some deterrent for the squirrels or fewer birds will arrive at feeders. A decision was made to feed birds and enjoy them. The squirrel is not a welcome addition in this tiny ecosystem. It is only the expense.

If you love feeding birds, but the squirrels are thwarting you, consider all the answers provided above. Providing generous amounts of seed and keeping it free from rain or snow will make your landscape a place of bird activity. According to authorities on barn feeders, or something similar on a pole, the only way to keep squirrels out is to have a sheet metal worker make an inverted cone to fit your feeder and pole. A little custom work is well worth this. The inverted sheet metal cone, at 45 degrees angled down the pole, is foolproof.

CHAPTER 6

Birds and Bugs

Birds work the whole summer long, suppressing insects. They aren't in complete control of the insect population, but they do keep the numbers down significantly.

The help of the birds in keeping control of the number of insects is understood and appreciated by farmers and other plant growers. Insect control by birds is often referred to as economic ornithology. This is certainly a form of integrated pest management, something the USDA has been developing for years. Information is difficult for the layman to come by. W. L. McAtee of the USDA, more than anyone else, assembled the most information on birds in relation to crop insect control. His philosophies about land are classic. He prefaced his words with caution pertaining to the extent of control to be expected from birds:

> *The general utility of birds in checking the increase of injurious animals and plants is well understood. It must be admitted, however, that while birds constantly exert a repressive influence on the numbers of the organisms they prey upon, and even exterminate certain pests, they are not numerous enough to cope successfully with widespread invasions.*
>
> *Birds are prone to feed upon things that are abundant and easily accessible.*

> *For instance, in elderberry season, a large number of birds take the berries.*
>
> *If mayflies swarm in a locality, practically all of the birds there devour them. Thus, under unusual conditions, such as attend outbreaks of insects or other pests, birds may very naturally turn their attention to the plentiful and easily obtained food intensified by the flocking of birds from surrounding areas.*

In the early days of settlement in Utah, the Mormon cricket threatened the food supply of the settlers. When seagulls came to their aid, it was considered to be an act of God, and in reality it was God's nature. The numbers of insects consumed by insectivore birds is probably astronomical.

About 1858, J. W. P. Jenks examined the stomachs of robins to learn something about their food habits and economic relationships to agriculture. This was pioneering work in pest management. The wild songbirds feed indiscriminately on whatever insects may be available; both injurious and beneficial insects are taken.

F. E. L. Beal, in the USDA Yearbook of 1908, helps us:

> *Whoever expects to find in birds beneficent organisms working with a sole view to the benefit of the human race will be doomed to disappointment. Birds eat food to sustain life and in their selection, they are also guided entirely by dietary considerations. As a whole, it is found that they eat insects of the various species in about the proportions in which these species exist in nature; it would appear that the true function of insectivorous birds is not so much to destroy this or*

> *that insect pest as it is to lessen the numbers of the insect tribe as a whole, to reduce to a lower level the great floodtide of insect life.*

In our bird ecology, our concern is not for crops. We just want insect eaters to have a good number of insects to eat. In the time of McAtee, insects thrived because there was little pollution and the birds could hardly keep up with the amount of insects. With declining numbers of insects, bird numbers also lessen. As the destructive insects are usually the most abundant ones, nature's role for birds is the best control we have.

In agricultural crops, the birds are not an adequate enough pest intercession to be economical. If they were, it would be a blessing. On the whole, their impact is spectacular, but not enough to be an adequate control when insects move in on crops. Crop losses can be devastating in a matter of days without timed sprays of insecticide.

Around the turn of the century, economic ornithology was established as a science. Work in control of insects was significant. Evidently, complete control of insects was a difficulty and not an economic possibility. It could be that insects were made for the birds rather than the birds being made to control the insects.

APPENDIX A

A Do's and Don'ts Guide for Beginning Bird Watchers

Look and listen—but don't touch.

DO . . . look and listen

Watch for birds around your home, school, or park.
What color is their body, breast, head, and wing?
What shape is their beak?
What shape are their wings and tail?
What size is the bird? Compare with a robin or crow.

Note where you see the bird.
Was it on the ground? In a tree? By a pond?
On a cliff? On a building?

Use a bird guide to try to identify the birds you see and hear.
Can you tell the male from the female?

Listen for the songs of birds.
Can you spot the bird that is singing?
Can you learn to recognize that bird by its song?

Find a nest to watch during the spring but don't get too close.
Can you see the bird collecting items for the nest?
Do both the male and female work on the nest?
Can you tell when the eggs have been laid?

Does a parent stay with the nest?

Can you tell when the eggs have hatched? Can you hear the young?

Be a friend to the birds.

Keep a bird feeder with seeds and suet or put out fruit, or fats (lard) but do not use bacon grease. HOWEVER, if you begin to feed the birds, you should continue. This is especially important in late winter and early spring when the birds have a hard time finding other food. Birds will quickly rely on the food you give them, and could be harmed if the food stops.

Keep a journal of the birds you see.

Make a note of the dates, times of day, and locations you see them.

What were they doing?

Make sketches showing the birds' behavior.

DON'T . . . touch.

Don't collect bird nests or feathers. Nests may be used again.

To protect these birds, it is against the law to collect nests and feathers.

Don't handle a baby bird even if you think it fell out of a nest and has been abandoned by its parents.

From the Connecticut Museum of Natural History, University of Connecticut, Storrs, CT

APPENDIX B

Attracting Hummingbirds

Feeding hummingbirds has long been a popular hobby in the western part of North America, where bird-watchers may see as many as eight different species at backyard feeders. Hummer feeding is also catching on in the East, even though only one species, the ruby-throated hummingbird, is generally seen there. If you haven't yet experienced the joys of backyard hummingbirding, here are a few tips to get you started.

Selecting a Feeder

Although you can attract seed-eating birds to your yard by scattering a handful of sunflower seeds on the ground, to bring hummers in, you need a special feeder, one that's designed to dispense a sugar solution similar to flower nectar, the hummer's principal food.

Hummingbird feeders need not be intricate or expensive, though. In fact, many people build their own from a bottle, a rubber cork, and a drinking tube like the ones used in hamster cages. But many fine feeders are commercially available. What features should you look for?

First, a hummingbird feeder should be easy to clean and easy to fill. Before you purchase a feeder, check to see that the fill hole is large and easy to open. Then take the feeder apart. Does it have hard-to-clean nooks and crannies, or does the design allow you to reach all the surfaces with a scrub brush? Glass feeders, although fragile, are easier to clean than plastic ones.

Also choose a feeder with some red parts—the color seems to attract hummers. Or enhance the attractiveness of a feeder yourself by painting the feeding ports with red enamel paint or nail polish, or by attaching red ribbons or plastic flowers.

Finally, your feeder should be fitted with bee guards—small plastic screens that fit over the feeder ports. They keep insects away from the sugar solution while still allowing the hummers to insert their long bills into the nectar. Be sure that the guards are firmly attached, so they won't pull off in high winds. If you plan to place your feeder in full sunlight, purchase a saucer-shaped, basin-style feeder. The feeders shaped like inverted bottles tend to leak when you hang them in the sun; as the air trapped at the top of the bottle warms up, it expands and squeezes the nectar out.

Placing the Feeder

Hang your feeder near some perching sites such as shrubs or trees. Choose a location that's protected from the wind—buffeting breezes can spill the sugar solution. We also recommend choosing a shady location because the sugar solution spoils quickly in hot sun. Hummers are bold, so don't be shy about hanging the feeder close to the window, where you can see it well. The feeders that attach to a window with suction cups provide excitingly close encounters.

If you've never seen any hummingbirds in your neighborhood, a feeder alone may not draw them in. Tie some red ribbons where they'll flutter in the breeze; better yet, plan ahead and plant some of the flowers that attract hummers. Plants with red, tube-shaped blooms, such as bee balm and trumpet vine, work well.

Filling the Feeder

It's easy to make your own sugar solution. In a small saucepan, add one-quarter cup of sugar to one cup of water. Bring the mixture to a boil, and then let it cool. Fill the feeder, and store any extra sugar solution in the refrigerator. The recipe may be doubled or tripled.

Use only ordinary table sugar in the solution, don't use honey—it promotes the growth of mold and bacteria. And don't add red food coloring—it just isn't necessary in a properly designed feeder.

Some folks worry that hummers will become malnourished on a diet of straight sugar water. They probably would, but your backyard hummers will supplement their feeder refreshments with plenty of small insects. The commercial hummingbird nectars with added vitamins and minerals are a needless expense.

Feeder Maintenance

To curb the growth of harmful molds and bacteria, make it a habit to clean your feeder every three days, even when temperatures are cool. (It's much easier to clean a feeder before it becomes totally black with mold than after.) Discard the old sugar solution, and then rinse the feeder well with hot water, using a bottlebrush to scrub any hard-to-reach places. Do not use soap or detergent. You can also clean your feeder by filling it with vinegar solution and some uncooked rice grains and shaking it vigorously.

You may find that your feeder attracts ants and bees. To discourage the ants, smear petroleum jelly on the feeder support pole, or try the device called "Ant Scat" (manufactured by Burd Corporation). It keeps ants off the feeder with a little moat of vegetable oil. If bees are a problem, try moving your feeder to a new location in your yard. The bees will lose track of it, at least for a while, but the hummingbirds will quickly find it again.

Hummingbirds are territorial and quite aggressive toward other hummingbirds. If you hang out a multiple-perch feeder, expecting to attract many hummers, you may find that a single male dominates it, defending his food supply with such vengeance that other birds cannot feed. If this happens (and if you want to see more than one hummingbird), try hanging out one of the feeders that has large plastic flowers disguising each feeding port. When the dominant hummer comes to feed, the "flower" may block his view of other hummingbirds, so that they can approach the feeder. Or, try setting out several feeders, positioning them so the aggressive bird can see only one or two at a time.

The table below tells you what hummingbird species you might see in your region. If you've never hung out a hummingbird feeder before, why not try it this summer? It will open up a whole new world of backyard birding.

Used with permission from the Cornell University, Cornell Laboratory of Ornithology, 159 Sapsucker Woods Road, Ithaca, NY 14850

Hummingbird Species by Region

East and Midwest	Western Midwest and Midwest	West Coast	Southwest (Common Species)
Ruby-throated	Black-chinned	Allen's	Allen's
	Broad-tailed	Anna's	Anna's
	Calliope	Black-chinned	Black-chinned
	Rufous	Broad-tailed	Blue-throated
		Calliope	Calliope
		Costa's	Costa's
		Rufous	Magnificent

APPENDIX C

Community Bird Refuges

W. L. McAtee

Bird Refuges on Farms

Farmers, more than any other element of the population, will be interested in the establishment and maintenance of effective bird refuges, for the welfare of crops and the commercial success of the farm are intimately related to the numbers and kinds of birds present and to their economic tendencies. In the case of certain species which are more or less injurious, control measures are sometimes necessary, but the great majority of birds vary from slightly to almost exclusively beneficial in their relations to the farm. The useful species merit the fullest protection and should be encouraged in every way.

The value of birds lies chiefly in their destruction of injurious insects. Leading an active life, they require much food, and are the most ravenous enemies of pests of this kind. The various groups of birds differ so much in habits that they feed upon practically all groups of insects; hardly an agricultural pest escapes their attacks. The alfalfa weevil has 45 different bird enemies; the army worm, 43; bill-bugs 67; cotton-boll weevil, 66; brown-tail moth, 31; chestnut weevils 64; chinch bug, 24; clover-root borers, 85; clover weevil, 25; codling moth, 36; cotton worm, 41; cutworms, 98; forest tent caterpillar, 43; potato beetle, 25; rice weevil, 21; seventeen-year locust, 38; twelve-spotted cucumber beetle, 28; white grubs, 67; and wireworms, 168.

In feeding on insect pests not only do birds take a great variety but they frequently destroy very large numbers. Often more than a hundred individuals are devoured at a meal, and in the case of small insects sometimes several thousand. With such appetites it is not surprising that occasionally birds entirely destroy certain insects locally. A number of cases are known in which trees, garden crops, and even farm fields have been entirely freed of insect pests by birds. On a two-hundred-acre farm in North Carolina it was found that birds were destroying a million green bugs, or wheat aphids, daily.

On the average there are in the United States only about two birds to the acre, but where they are protected and encouraged it has been demonstrated that a very great increase over the normal bird population can be secured. No fewer than fifty-nine pairs to the acre is the figure reached in the most successful of these attempts reported. At an estimated value of ten cents each—a figure ridiculously low, but used to insure a safe minimum estimate—the birds of the United States prevent an increase in the annual damage done by insects of more than $400,000,000.

A particular farm may not have so large a bird population as it should and therefore may not be deriving the benefit which is its due. The most effective means of increasing the number of birds is protection in its best sense, afforded by the establishment of bird refuges.

Bird refuges on farms have been most successful when established and maintained on a cooperative plan between the landowner or landowners and a state game commission, an Audubon society, a bird club, or a school. The owner agrees to the use of the land and acts as warden, and the other party to the contract furnishes and places posters, birdhouses, and feeding stations, or even stocks the refuge, as in the case of reservations for game birds. The beneficial effect which the establishment of a bird refuge has upon trespass problems is a great advantage to the farmer. A state law authorizing game wardens to proceed against trespassers on bird reservations greatly increases the effectiveness of private and cooperative bird refuges.

The cooperative bird reserve has been tried in many states as a means of establishing colonies of game birds, such as pheasants, and the plan has invariably proved popular and successful. As a method of protecting insectivorous birds it has been put into practice by schools, bird clubs, and Audubon societies in New Hampshire, Connecticut, Illinois, and Minnesota, at least, and has been found satisfactory and effective.

In creating a useful bird refuge, the first step is to insure adequate protection against all bird enemies; the second, to see that plenty of nesting sites suited to the needs of various birds are available; and the third, to improve food and water supplies, if necessary. Instructions for accomplishing these results are contained in five earlier Farmers' bulletins, of which No. 1456 adapted to the whole country, relates to birdhouses; and the following four, to methods of attracting birds in various parts of the country: 621, Northeastern States; 760, Northwestern States; 844, Middle Atlantic States; and 912, East Central States.

Roadsides

Making bird refuges on farms, while of most direct interest to the farmer, is by no means the only activity along this line helpful to agriculture. Attracting birds to roadsides and right-of-ways, in particular, is of almost equal importance, and furnishes a leading reason for urging a treatment of these public and semipublic travel ways that will not only increase their bird population but make them more sightly. Both features will increase the value of the adjacent farms.

There exists in most parts of the United States either a superstition, a conviction, or a legal requirement that roadsides be shorn of their vegetation at least once a year. The result is that most country roads are very uninviting in summer. Hot and gray with dust, the highway stretches away before the traveler, often without a single tree to break the monotony of the view or afford relief from the rays of the sun. This baldness is brought about chiefly by two causes: (1) Fear that the roadside will unduly increase weeds and insect and rodent pests; and (2) lack of public spirit.

Fortunately, we also have in this country examples of well-kept parkways and boulevards which border cultivated lands. Their ample parking is grown to grass and embellished with herbaceous flowering plants, shrubs, and trees. Yet the farmlands they border are neither overwhelmed by weeds nor devastated by insects and rodents.

The question of roadsides propagating vast numbers of noxious weeds may be viewed in more than one light. For instance, the mowing of waysides for long series of years has not done away with the need of cultivating adjacent crops; indeed it cannot, for cultivation is necessary for other reasons than the destruction of weeds, as loosening, aeration, and water conservation. Furthermore, the amount of cultivation customarily given crops is sufficient to control all the weeds the land will grow, and this number is generally present, despite the razing of roadside growths. On the other hand, the lack of verdure and shade and the general dreariness of roadsides make the adoption of a different treatment of these most extensive public parkings very desirable. Placing vines upon fences and planting numerous shrubs and shade trees along the way will not only render the roads more attractive but will tend to keep down the dust.

In the case of paved highways it has recently been demonstrated also that roadside trees prolong the life of the pavement by protecting it from extremes of temperature. This is particularly true of the heat of summer, which, depending on the nature of the pavement, may either expand it, causing the surface to be thrown into waves, or dry it out, forming cracks.

Another practical end of planting may be served by using nutbearing trees, which could be made a definite source of revenue to the community. In choosing plants for roadsides, as elsewhere, be sure to omit the common barberry, which serves as an alternate host for wheat rust; gooseberries and currants, which have a similar relation to the white pine blister rust; and the wild cherry, which is a favorable nursery for tent caterpillars.

There can be no doubt that suppression of roadside vegetation is a potent factor in restricting the numbers of birds, and the ever increasing tendency to allow fence rows the minimum of space has the same effect. Farmers may gain a planting row about every field by the destruction of vegetation along fences, but they love the services of the birds, their best allies in fighting insects.

Shrubby fence rows are among the best harbors and nesting places of small birds, and it is certain that encouraging an abundance of birds to live on farms by such plantings is a profitable policy. More should be done to beautify roadsides and fence rows, not only as a measure to contribute to the comfort and pleasure of man, but also to substantially increase a great economic asset—the bird population of the country.

In effect, windbreaks, so useful on farms in prairie regions, are but shrubby fence rows, magnified. Their utility in protecting crops from wind always is supplemented by that of furnishing nesting sites for birds, and a food-supplying function also may easily be added, since Russian olive, buffaloberry, and hackberry, all good bird foods, are highly recommended for windbreaks.

Right-of-Ways

A number of railroad companies have already made considerable effort to beautify their right-of-ways and station grounds. In some places the roads are paralleled for many miles by hedges, and the land on either side of the tracks is covered by beautiful turf. Hedges, shrubbery, and flower beds are common about the stations. If this planting could be directed in part, at least, toward attracting birds, it would be very effective and great good would be done. If the clumps of shrubs were formed of kinds furnishing bird food and more of them were placed along the right-of-ways, the hedges allowed to bear fruit, and the fence poles or possibly even some of the telegraph poles furnished with birdhouses, thousands of birds could live where very few do now.

The suggestions made are by no means without practical value to the right-of-way itself. For instance, supplying bird boxes is the best method of preventing damage to poles by woodpeckers, which come anyway under present conditions and make their own homes. Hedges or fences densely covered with vines would decrease, if not entirely obviate, expenditures for the movable snow fences now extensively used.

Community Parkings

The attractiveness of community parkings, including those of cities and villages as well as of rural areas, may well be increased by the presence of an abundance of birds. This can be effected without in any way detracting from the utility of these reservations for their leading purposes. Making community parkings safe for birds is the first step; they must actually be havens of refuge. In this connection may be cited the admirable law of the State of Oregon, which provides that all incorporated towns and cities and all public parks and school grounds in the state shall be, without additional local or general legislation, bird and game sanctuaries.

Municipal Parks and Picnic and Fair Grounds

Picnic grounds, fair grounds, and parks may be improved as places of public gatherings, recreation, and education by increasing their bird population. Moreover, the alterations that improve a park as a bird haven may, and should, themselves be made to add to its attractiveness. For instance, water is used to enhance the beauty of most parks, and a water supply is one the most potent attractions for birds. Bird baths or bird fountains may take the form of small displays of water, which may be added to many parks without being obtrusive or in conflict with the general design.

An artistic martin house, well placed in one of the small open lawns that most large parks contain, would not only increase the beauty and interest of the park, but would add to its dignity by suggesting a specific usefulness for the space. As for nest boxes for other birds, they may be so inconspicuously placed that the chief evidence of their presence would be the increased number of birds and the lessened injury to vegetation by insect pests. The perfection of specimen trees in parks and the work of the tree surgeon on imperfect trees make it necessary to supply nest boxes if the hole-nesting birds are to have any chance of inhabiting parks.

Feeding stations for birds are made in a number of sightly designs, and the principles upon which they are built allow of their being extensively varied and incorporated into other park structures. The greatest usefulness of feeding stations in parks, aside from the preservation of birds, is in rendering such places more attractive to the public in winter. The feeding of birds is carried on with most obvious results during the colder months, and adding this feature to parks appeals strongly to thousands of lovers of nature.

By means of feeding stations it is possible to attract to convenient observation points several species of the most interesting and valuable birds. Such stations are particularly pleasing to children. As evidence of the value of the method, the following statement of experience by Theodore Wirth, Superintendent of Parks, Minneapolis, Minn., is presented:

> *For the past five or six years we have maintained a number of feeding stations in various parts of our park system, with very satisfactory results. I give you a list of the birds which stay with us over winter. The permanent winter birds found in the vicinity of our parks are the chickadee, blue jay, white-breasted nuthatch, downy and hairy woodpeckers, and screech owl; winter visitors, the redpoll, tree sparrow, and junco; irregular winter visitors, the evening grosbeak, Bohemian waxwing, and snow bunting. It is safe to say that a large number of these species are staying in the parks on account of the food supplied them. The feeding of the wild birds in the parks is a great success and will be continued.*

Supplying water, nest boxes, and winter food goes far toward making a bird haven, but it is important also to supplement the summer food. This can best be done by planting fruit-bearing shrubs and trees. Shrubs and trees are essential elements of park composition, but according to the judgment of bird lovers better choice is distinctly possible than that often made.

The guiding principle in park planning should be beauty, but it should not be a temporary or one-seasonal beauty. Hence it follows that shrubs and trees which produce colored fruits and retain them for long periods are preferable to plants whose chief decorative contribution is a short burst of bloom. Such shrubs are handsomer at all times after flowering and are particularly valuable in winter when every bit of color in the landscape is precious. They are valuable, moreover, in supplying bird food.

A few further suggestions as to the use of fruit-producing plants are not out of place. The ideal American park is natural woodland, modified and embellished, or a planting that follows natural lines. Informal treatment is almost universally preferred to formal. From the standpoint of bird attraction this is fortunate, since clipping shrubs either prevents or reduces the production of fruit and causes the plants to form such solid and dense surfaces that they are uninviting to birds. It may further be said in favor of untrimmed shrubbery that the normal form and beauty of the plants, together with the resultant play of light and motion, are preserved. With this treatment a park has naturalness and life; under formal treatment the suggestions are those of restraint and immobility.

School and College Grounds

Too often public-schools are bare and uninviting. How much better to clothe, shade, and adorn them with green. Flowers and trees will make the students more content with their surroundings inspire them to better work, and enshrine the school grounds in pleasant memories delightful to recall in later years. Almost everything done to beautify the grounds will help to attract birds. Trees and shrubs cradle their young and supply much of their food.

The birds, the trees, and the flowers in themselves are a valuable educational resource, and are necessities for the proper conduct of classes in nature study, now deservedly so popular. Building and placing birdhouses could well be part of such a course, and the winter feeding of the birds would attract living objects of interest during the dormant season of the trees and shrubs. All children like birds and will protect and encourage them if only their early steps are guided right.

The college campus, like the park, has suffered from formal landscape gardening. Wall-like hedges, closely cropped circles, triangles of shrubs, and mathematically designed edgings, beds, and gardens have gone far toward robbing school grounds of merit in the eyes of man, and have almost spoiled them for birds.

In campus planning it is desirable to take the birds into consideration for the same reasons as in park planning. In addition there is the very important objective of keeping up an important educational resource. There is hardly an advanced school in the country that does not offer one or more courses of bird study. The study of birds out-of-doors is essential to a good bird course, and this need should be kept in view by those in charge of college and school grounds. Sylvan campuses where formerly birds abounded have been so filled with buildings, so gardened and formalized, that birds are now scarce. If possible, some corner (preferably of original woodland, where that exists) should be allowed to run wild. Judicious addition of food-producing plants should be made there, and the campus in general improved for birds by allowing shrubs to make natural growths. Putting up nest boxes would make up for the hole-eliminating activities and instructive to many students and could be carried on as part of the course of bird-study classes. Finally, the teacher of ornithology might well have an advisory capacity in relation to the planning and treatment of the campus.

Cemeteries

Cemeteries have the reputation of being good places for birds. The reasons, one must infer are seclusion, freedom from disturbance, and an abundance of trees and shrubs. The last-named factor is by no means least, nor, on the other hand, so satisfactory as not to be susceptible of improvement. Selection of shrubs and trees with the needs of birds in mind not only would not interfere with the general plan of a cemetery, but would make it a still better resort for birds.

Formal landscape gardening is more prevalent (perhaps excusably so) in cemeteries than in other public reservations, yet there are very beautiful cemeteries in which formal composition plays little part. Here, as everywhere, the informal or naturalistic planting is most favorable to birds. Nest boxes can be added without being obtrusive, and bird fountains may be made to harmonize with the surrounding or even to serve as memorials.

The movement to convert cemeteries into bird sanctuaries and to improve them for the purpose is already well under way and is being fostered by the National Association Audubon Societies. A pioneer in this work, H.S. Mann, Secretary of the Forest Lawn Cemetery Association of Omaha, Nebr., reports:

> *We have been very successful in attracting birds to Forest Lawn Cemetery. The cemetery contains 320 acres, all fenced, and is located north of the city limits of greater Omaha. It has an abundance of trees and shrubbery, about 250 acres of the half section being unimproved at this time. A creek runs through the southern portion of the cemetery, and east and north of it are great stretches of wild lands.*
>
> *Birdhouses, feeding stations, and baths have been erected in the cemetery. Quantities of tangled underbrush and small fruit-bearing bushes and vines have been set out and preserved for the birds. With these attractions, free from annoyance of cats, hunters, and children at play, it is a paradise for birds.*
>
> *Bird students visit the cemetery frequently, as a larger number and a greater variety of birds may be found within its sacred inclosures than anywhere else in this section of the country, excepting perhaps in the great Fontenelle Forest Reserve of 2,500 acres on the Missouri River adjoining the city on the south.*

Reservoirs

The grounds surrounding reservoirs of drinking water usually are well fenced and carefully guarded to minimize contamination. This results in freedom from disturbance, a boon so highly appreciated by birds that in itself it goes far toward making these places satisfactory bird havens. Such reservations can be greatly improved for this purpose, however, by the use of birdhouses and by proper planting, measures which will be in no way deleterious to the water supply, but which will greatly benefit the birds and through them the vegetation of the reserve and of the adjacent country.

Reservoirs other than for drinking water usually can be sown to aquatic plants, thus making them attractive to many water birds. The character of the planting will depend on circumstances; if a marshy margin is permissible, the place may be made into an excellent resort for wild fowl. If only submerged plants are desired and as clean a growth as possible, sago pondweed may be planted. Broader leaved plants furnish much greater surface for the lodgment of silt and the growth of algae. The methods of propagating a variety of aquatic plants for the use of wild fowl are described in publications of the Department of Agriculture.

Golf Courses

There are numerous public golf courses, and many of those established by clubs are so surrounded by residences of members as to become virtually community institutions. Golfers as a class are broadly interested in the out of doors, including its animal inhabitants, and most of them no doubt will be glad to cooperate in the preservation, encouragement, and increase of useful birds. In fact, considering the well-known utility of birds in destroying insect and other pests, golf clubs will only be consulting their own interests in preserving and propagating these natural enemies of the foes of their greens and fairways.

Golf courses without special modification present several features that are attractive to birds. The broad expanses of short grass on the fairways furnish excellent feeding grounds for robins, meadowlarks, starlings, flickers, and killdeers. The longer grasses and weeds of the rough, and scattered clumps of trees and shrubbery open to full light, support an abundant insect population, an important source of food for our feathered friends. Many birds find nesting sites also in the arborescent growths present and sally forth for food over the grassed areas, where they are often joined by numbers of those aerial feeders, the swallows and swifts, which find on these unobstructed reaches happy hunting grounds.

Such are the impressions recalled of a season's observations on a golf course well-situated for birds. There are courses not so fortunate, but all have the fundamentals of valuable bird refuges. Protected to a considerable extent from trespass and relatively free from the natural enemies of birds, golf courses already have much of the safety required for sanctuaries. Birds promptly respond to protection; but it should be as complete as possible. So far as food is concerned, insects are plentiful on most golf courses, but it would help the birds and ornament the courses if shrubbery on the grounds were selected chiefly from species producing fruits fed upon by birds. Most golf courses, again, have water hazards at which birds can drink and bathe; but where these are absent or are far apart, bird fountains could easily be attached to hydrant supply pipes. These not only would be a boon to birds on hot summer days, but if placed in view of rest benches would be a source of interest and entertainment to members and visitors.

Protection, food, water—these are the things that usually are present to some degree and which may very easily be supplemented; but nesting sites, especially for some of the most useful birds, are scarce or lacking on most golf courses. Trees and shrubbery (the latter best if in tangled masses) will accommodate many birds; but that birds that nest in cavities can hardly find a home on improved lands, especially where tree-surgeons have been employed. Fortunately these birds will occupy artificial cavities or nest boxes.

In most cases nest boxes must be supplied if we would enliven and benefit our golf courses with such beautiful and useful birds as the purple martin, bluebird, house wren, tree swallow, flicker, white-breasted nuthatch, and chickadee. At least twice as many other kinds of small birds have been known to occupy nest boxes. Placing nest boxes is work which can well be done in winter, a season during which, at least on northern courses, employees are but little occupied, and when members may welcome something to do out of doors. Names of dealers in bird boxes, bird baths, and the like and bulletins treating all phases of bird attraction methods as well as advice in special cases, may be obtained by application to the Biological Survey. U.S. Department of Agriculture, Washington, D.C.

APPENDIX D

Providing Nest Sites for Backyard Birds

When you're choosing a place to install a nest box, location is everything. You can have the best-designed nest box in the world, but if it's set up in the wrong kind of habitat or at the wrong height from the ground for a given bird species, you'll never be able to get that species to nest in it.

The table provided, tells you how to position a nest box to attract each of thirty common cavity-nesting bird species found in North America. Factors to consider besides the type of habitat include the distance from the nest box to feeding sites and the availability of protective cover and perching sites.

Setting Up a Nest Box

You can use wood screws to attach your nest boxes to posts. We don't recommend using screws to mount nest boxes on living trees, however, because they will injure the tree. Eventually the wood surrounding the screws will decay, allowing the box to work loose. It's better to attach nest boxes to trees using coat-hanger wire wrapped around the trunk. (Cut a piece of old garden hose in half lengthwise and slip it between the wire and the bark for padding.) Make sure that the nest box is secure enough to withstand high winds and severe weather.

Many birds find a nest box most attractive if it has two to three inches of wood chips in the bottom. Species that prefer to excavate their own nest holes, such as some chickadees and woodpeckers, will use a nest box if it's packed full of wood chips so they can dig it out to suit their tastes. The right-hand column in the following table shows which species prefer wood chips and how much you should place in your nest box.

Where to Place Your Nest Box

Species	Habitat Code (see below)	Height (ft.) Above Ground or Water (w)	Wood Chips
Wood Duck	5, 10	12-18	+
Common Goldeneye	3, 5	4-20	+
Barrow's Goldeneye	3, 5	4-20	+
Bufflehead	3, 5	10-20	+
Hooded Merganser	3, 5	4-6	+
Common Merganser	3, 5	8-20	+
American Kestrel	1, 4	10-30	+
Barred Owl	5	15-20	+
Screech Owl	2	10-30	+
Boreal Owl	8	10-25	+
Saw-Whet Owl	2	12-20	+
Red-Headed Woodpecker	2	10-20	√
Golden-Fronted Woodpecker	2	10-20	√
Downy Woodpecker	2	5-15	√
Hairy Woodpecker	2	12-20	√
Northern Flicker	1, 2	6-30	√
Great-Crested Flycatcher	1, 2	8-20	
Ash-Throated Flycatcher	1, 6	10-20	+
Purple Martin	1	4-15	-
Tree Swallow	1, 9	4-15	-
Violet-Green Swallow	1, 9	4-15	-
Chickadees	2	5-15	+
Titmice	2	5-10	+
Nuthatches	2	5-10	√
Carolina Wren	2, 7	5-10	-
Bewicks Wren	2, 7	5-10	-
House Wren	2, 7	4-10	-
Bluebirds	1, 9	3-6	-
Prothonotary Warbler	3, 5	4-12, 3w	-

Habitat Codes

1. Open areas in the sun (not permanently shaded by trees), pastures, fields, or golf courses.
2. Woodland clearings or edge of woods.
3. Above water, or if on land, with the entrance facing away from water.
4. On trunks of large trees or poles in open fields.
5. Moist forest bottomlands, flooded river valleys, or swamps.
6. Semiarid country, deserts, dry open woods, and wood edges.
7. Backyards, near buildings.
8. Mixed conifer-hardwood forests.
9. Mount box on post facing and within 50 feet of a tree, fence, or other structure. Keep away from bushy hedgerows. Mount multiple boxes at least 100 yards apart.
10. Near water, well hidden in tree canopy and out of sight of other boxes.

Wood Chip Key

+	Add 2-3" of wood shavings or chips to box.
√	Fill box completely with packed wood shavings or chips.
-	Do not add wood chips.

Don't be discouraged if birds don't use your nest box right away. Boxes often become attractive to birds only after they've been up for a season or two.

Setting Up a Nest Shelf

Several species of birds like to build their nests under the sheltered eaves of houses and outbuildings. If nesting American robins, barn swallows, or eastern phoebes are making a mess of your front porch, you can entice them to nest in a more convenient location by providing a nest shelf.

Many of the companies that sell nest boxes also carry nest shelves. Be sure to attach the shelf in a place that's not too close to busy doorways, porches, or decks. These shelves are easy to clean and will allow you and your family to watch the birds' entire nesting cycle.

Other Considerations

Once you have installed your box or shelf and the birds start building their nests, you may want to provide them with nesting materials. A variety of songbirds use the following items in their nest building:

String	Yarn
Down	Straw
Soft nonsynthetic cloth strips	Bark
Fur	Moss
Wool	Wood shavings
Unraveled rope	Thread

Cut materials into three- to four-inch lengths and set them out on the ground near the box or hang them over a bush or in the crotch of a tree. Wrens will also use twigs broken into short lengths.

(Used with permission from the Cornell University, Cornell Laboratory of Ornithology, 159 Sapsucker Woods Road, Ithaca, NY 14850)

Birdhouse Specifications

Species	Floor (inches)	Front (inches)	Entrance Above Floor (inches)	Diameter Entrance Hole (inches)	Actual Board Thickness (inches)	Top (inches)	Side (inches)	Side (inches)
Wood Duck	10×12	22	17	4×3	1	16	24	27
Common Goldeneye	12×12	24	20	5	1	16	26	29
Barrow's Goldeneye	9×9	30	24	4	1	13	32	35
Bufflehead	7×7	16	13	2 7/8	1	11	18	21
Hooded Merganser	10×10	18	13	5	1	14	20	23
Common Merganser	11×11	40	35	5	1	14	20	23
American Kestrel	8×8	15	12	3	3	12	17	20
Barred Owl	12×12	24	14	6	1	16	26	29
Screech Owl	8×8	15	11	3	1	12	17	20
Boreal Owl	7×7	18	14	2 1/2×5	1	11	20	23
Saw-Whet Owl	6×6	12	8	2 1/2	3/4	9 1/2	14	17
Red-Headed Woodpecker	6×6	12	9	2	3/4	9 1/2	14	17
Golden-Fronted Woodpecker	6×6	12	9	2	3/4	9 1/2	14	17
Downy Woodpecker	4×4	9	7	1 1/4	3/4	7 1/2	10	14
Hairy Woodpecker	6×6	15	12	1 5/8	3/4	9 1/2	17	20
Northern Flicker	7×7	18	14	2 1/2	1	11	20	23
Great-Crested Flycatcher	6×6	10	8	1 9/16*	3/4	9 1/2	11	15
Ash-Throated Flycatcher	6×6	10	8	1 1/2	3/4	9 1/2	11	15
Purple Martin	6×6	6	1	2 1/4	3/4	9 1/2	7	11
Tree Swallow	5×5	10	7	1 1/2*	3/4	8 1/2	11	15
Violet-Green Swallow	5×5	10	7	1 1/2*	3/4	8 1/2	11	15
Chickadees	4×4	9	7	1 1/8	3/4	7 1/2	10	14
Titmice	4×4	9	7	1 1/4	3/4	7 1/2	10	14
Brown Headed & Pygmy Nuthatches	4×4	9	7	1 1/8	3/4	7 1/2	10	14
Red-Breasted Nuthatch	4×4	9	7	1 1/4	3/4	7 1/2	10	14
White-Breasted Nuthatch	4×4	9	7	1 3/8	3/4	7 1/2	10	14
Carolina Wren	4×4	8	6	1 1/2*	3/4	7 1/2	9	13
Bewick's Wren	4×4	8	6	1 1/2	3/4	7 1/2	9	13
House Wren	4×4	8	6	1 1/4	3/4	7 1/2	9	13
Eastern Blubird & Western Bluebird	4×4	10	6 1/2	1 1/2*	3/4	7 1/2	11	15
Mountain Bluebird	4×4	10	7	1 9/16*	3/4	7 1/2	11	15
Prothonotary Warbler	4×4	6	4	1 3/8	3/4	7 1/2	7	11

*Precise measurements required; if diameter is larger, starlings may take over box.

APPENDIX E

Where to Study Ornithology

So you want to become an ornithologist. You're applying to college, and you're wondering, "What are the best schools for studying ornithology?" But you've looked in the College Blue Book and other sources of information about colleges and haven't found the word *ornithology*.

It may seem surprising that information about studying birds is harder to find than the birds themselves! The problem is that no university or college in North America has an "ornithology" major. But that doesn't mean you can't study ornithology. This will give you some hints for choosing a school that will allow you to pursue your interest, whether you are a high school senior contemplating college or a career-changer who is investigating graduate schools.

The field of ornithology is a diverse as biology itself. As the American Ornithologists Union puts it, "Ornithologists are biologists that specialize in the study of birds." Some ornithologists may be interested in bird behavior, others in increases and decreases of bird populations, and still others in the anatomy and physiology of birds. But all ornithologists have three characteristics in common: They have a strong background in biology, a special knowledge in one area of biology, and an intense interest in birds.

Ornithologists receive their training in a variety of ways. Most pursue degrees at the many reputable universities around the globe. Others forego institutional education and pursue their interest in birds through intense fieldwork on their own.

What to Look for

What should you look for in a school if you want to study ornithology? First and foremost, the school must have faculty members who are actively doing research on birds. These professors can help students gain experience in research, guide them in their course work, and provide contacts with ornithologists at other institutions. A faculty member can also help students publish their research in scientific journals—a "feather in the cap" for the student's academic and professional future.

To find out whether the school you are considering includes ornithologists on its faculty, write to the department of biology, zoology, or natural resources and ask for a list of the faculty and their research interests.

Second, the best colleges and universities for bird study have large collections of study skins or museum specimens. A skin collection is an invaluable resource for bird study. It also is a great source of ideas for research projects, which are required in most biology courses. Correlating wing shape with migratory distance or measuring variations in bill length are two examples of research projects that can be accomplished with a skin collection.

Used with permission from the Cornell University, Cornell Laboratory of Ornithology, 159 Sapsucker Woods Road, Ithaca, NY 14850

APPENDIX F

Attracting and Managing Purple Martins

Over one million North Americans put up housing for purple martins. Unfortunately, many of these folks are unable to attract breeding martins. The advice given here will increase your chances of attracting martins. Once martins nest at your location, they will come back every year, if you manage the site properly.

Landlords who lose their entire colony from one year to the next often suspect their "flock" died in a storm during migration or was poisoned by pesticides on their wintering grounds. These scenarios are unlikely; the martins that share a breeding site do not migrate or overwinter as a colony. The reason for total colony loss is most often the result of something that happened in the landlord's own backyard, during the nesting season. Good management practices can prevent or minimize most of these problems.

Location

The major reason people fail to attract martins is that martin housing is not placed correctly, or their site is inappropriate martin habitat to begin with. Martins have very specific aerial space requirements. Housing should be placed in the center of the most open spot available, about thirty to one hundred feet from human housing. There should be no trees taller than the martin housing within forty feet, preferably sixty feet. Generally, the farther the housing is placed from trees, the better. In the southern half of their breeding range, martins are less particular about house placement. Southern landlords can sometimes place housing within fifteen to twenty feet of trees, and still attract martins. Height of the housing can be anywhere from ten to twenty feet. Keep tall bushes, shrubs, and vines away from the pole. Do not attach wires to a martin house, especially if they lead to trees, buildings, or to the ground. If your yard has too many trees near the martin housing, relocate the housing to a more open area, mount the housing higher, or prune (or remove) trees to create a more open site.

Timing

Most "would-be" martin landlords rush to get their martin housing opened up for the arrival of martin "scouts" in their particular area. This is four to five weeks too early for new sites, and decreases chances for success. Contrary to popular folklore, "scouts" are not looking for new breeding sites for their flocks. "Scouts" are simply the first martins to arrive in, or pass through, an area on their way back to their previous year's nesting sites. These martins aren't likely to switch to new housing. Prospective landlords should not open their housing until about four weeks after the first martins are scheduled to return to their area. No matter where you live, keep your housing open through June. Martins may arrive and begin nesting as late as the end of June, anywhere in North America. Landlords of active sites can leave their housing completely closed up until the martins return and land on the housing. Purple martins exhibit a very high level of site fidelity—once they have bred successfully at a specific location, the same individuals return to breed there year after year.

Competition

If any other species is allowed to claim unoccupied martin housing, martins are not likely to stay. All birds set up territories around their nest sites and defend them against other birds. When [English] house sparrows or European starlings lay first claim to unoccupied martin housing, they fill the compartments with their nests, chase off investigating martins, fight with nesting martins, kill nestlings, and break eggs. Allowing house sparrows and starlings to nest in martin housing will significantly reduce martin occupancy and productivity. Controlling nest-site competitors may require repeated lowerings of the house for nest tear-outs, and in the case of the nonnative house sparrow and european starling, trapping and/or shooting. The starling-proof entrance hole can be used to keep starlings from claiming martin housing. Should native bird species (e.g., tree swallow, eastern bluebird, great crested flycatcher, etc.) try to take over your empty martin housing, temporarily plug all the entrance holes with door stops or paper cups, then put up appropriate, single-unit housing elsewhere on your property. Once they have accepted the new housing, reopen the martin housing. Housing should be stored inside for the winter, or closed up, to keep paper wasps, squirrels, and other birds from claiming the house before the martins return.

Housing

Houses and gourds should be painted white, or a light pastel color; trim can be any color. White housing seems to attract martins best. White housing reflects the heat of the sun, keeping nestlings cooler.

Compartment floor dimensions should measure at least six by six inches, but seven by twelve offers better protection against predators and weather, if starlings are controlled. Compartment height can be from 4½-inches to six to seven inches. Place entrance holes about one inch above the floor. Hole size can range from 1¾-inches up to 2¼-inches. Many published plans for martin housing, and some manufactured houses, are made to improper dimensions, so if your housing is unsuccessful, check the dimensions, and modify where needed.

Look for housing designed to raise and lower vertically, and with easy access to compartments. Landlords may need to lower housing daily to evict nest-site competitors, or to check on martin nestlings.

Systems that telescope up and down, or raise and lower with a pulley and winch, are the most practical. Nest checks will not cause martins to abandon their nests or their colony site; number the compartments and keep written records.

Replacing Active Housing

The same martins return each year, and may abandon the site if the housing they are used to is gone, or drastically altered. To safely replace a single active house, place the new housing near the housing you plan to remove, and give the martins an entire season to get used to it. Do not remove the active housing until some of the martins have accepted and bred in the new housing for at least one season. Once martins have nested in the new housing, you can remove the old house, or put an additional new house in its place. Landlords with several active houses can replace a house between seasons without risk of colony loss.

Predation

The most common reason martins abandon their colony site is because predators have raided their nests. It only takes one foray up a martin pole by a snake, raccoon, or squirrel, or a few visits by an owl, hawk, or crow, to cause all the surviving birds to abandon the site. Landlords who don't conduct weekly nest checks may never know their martins, nestlings, or eggs are disappearing. All martin poles (wooden or metal) can easily be climbed by predators and should be equipped with pole-guards. Martin houses that have become regular targets for hawks, owls, or crows should be equipped with owl guards. Landlords should be alert for evidence of predation (e.g., dropped owl feathers, plucked martin feathers, chewed-off martin wings, etc.) under martin housing.

Weather Extremes

Since martins feed solely on flying insects, they are extremely vulnerable to weather conditions that affect insect availability. Prolonged bad weather, such as rain, snow, cool temperatures, and/or heavy winds, all reduce or eliminate insect flight. If poor weather persists for more than four or five days, martins begin to die of starvation. Heat waves and droughts can also be a problem. When air temperatures go above one hundred degrees Fahrenheit for many days, nestlings can perish from overheating. Prolonged drought can also adversely affect insect numbers. Some weather conditions may contribute to a population explosion of some external parasites normally found in martin nests, including fleas, nest mites, and blowfly larvae. Never use pesticides in bird nests or boxes. The safe way to reduce numbers of nest parasites is to remove nest material (and nestlings), sprinkle one or two teaspoons of freshwater diatomaceous earth over the floor, then replace the old nest material with clean, dry wood shavings, pine straw (dried pine needles), or dry straw. Shape a shallow bowl in the material, and place the nestlings back in the nest.

Used with permission of Purple Martin Conservation Association, Edinboro University of Pennsylvania

APPENDIX G

Sources

American Primitive Gallery
596 Broadway, Suite 205
New York, NY 10012
(212) 966-1530
Extensive selection of vintage and new folk-art birdhouses

Art Effect
934 West Armitage
Chicago, IL 60614
(773) 929-3600
Birdhouses, home accessories

Birdwatchers General Store
36 Route 6A
Orleans, MA 02653
(508) 255-6974
Wide selection of bird-friendly houses and feeders

Carmel Bay Company
P.O. Box 5606
Ocean Avenue and Lincoln Street
Carmel, CA 93921
(831) 624-3868
Home furnishings, rustic birdhouses

Dakota Quality Bird Feed
Box 3084
Fargo, ND 58108
(800) 356-9220
Seed, feeders, feed houses

Devonshire
P.O. Box 1860
Main Street
Bridgehampton, NY 11932
(631) 537-2661
Decorative accessories for home and garden, birdhouses

Discovery Channel Store
2 Explore Lane
P.O. Box 788
Florence, KY 41022
(800) 227-1114
Paraphernalia for naturalists, including birdhouses, bird feeders, optical equipment, books

Droll Yankee Inc.
27 Mill Road
Foster, RI 02825
(401) 647-3324
Feeders, hooks, books

Duncraft
11 Fisherville Road
Penacook, NH 03303
(603) 224-0200
Seed, feed, feeders, houses, books, telescoping poles, manufacturers of National Audubon Society products

Flights of Fancy
1502 1st Avenue
New York, NY 10021
(212) 772-1302
Decorative rustic birdhouses and feeders

The Gardener
1836 Fourth Street
Berkeley, CA 94710
(510) 548-4545
Home and garden, birdhouses and supplies

Gardener's Eden
Mail Order Department
1655 Bassford Drive
Mexico, MO 65265
(800) 822-9600
Birdhouses

Georgica Creek Antiques
P.O. Box 877
Montauk Highway
Wainscott, NY 11975
(631) 537-0333
Antique large-scale birdhouses

La Ruche
168 Newbury Street
Boston, MA 02116
(617) 536-6366
Birdhouses, garden ornaments, decorative accessories

Lazy Hill Farms
P.O. Box 235
Colerain, NC 27924
(252) 356-2828
Cedar and cypress birdhouses and feeders in traditional styles, including shingle-roofed English dovecotes

Lexington Gardens
1011 Lexington Avenue
New York, NY 10021
(212) 861-4390
Birdhouses, garden ornaments

Maine Manna
P.O. Box 248
Gorham, ME 04038
(207) 839-6013
Suet and seed bells, dispensers

Massachusetts Audubon Shop
South Great Road
Lincoln, MA 01773
(781) 259-9661
Houses, kits and nesting shelves for 11 species

Chris Mead's English Country Antiques
Snake Hollow Road
Bridgehampton, NY 11932
(631) 537-4725
Rustic birdhouses

Meta Nature Products
c/o Tim Linquist
56 Walkers Hill
Tivoli, NY 12583
(518) 828-0533
Information on ordering estate wild bird feeder

Old Elm Feed and Supplies
Box 825
13400 Watertown Plank Road
Elm Grove, WI 53122
(800) 782-3300
Seed, feeders, feed, houses

Pastime Antiques
Box 102
Highway 190
Jamesport, MO 64648
(660) 684-6222
Birdhouses

Remington Freeman Ltd.
225 Fifth Avenue
New York, NY 10010
(212) 689-5542
Distributors of a variety of rustic and other birdhouses

The Sampler
96 Summit Avenue
Summit, NJ 07901
(908) 277-4747
Wide selection of decorative birdhouses and a display of vintage birdhouses

Nancy Thomas Gallery
145 Ballard Street
Yorktown, VA 23690
(757) 898-3665
New and antique folk art, birdhouses and accessories

Wild Bird Centers of America, Inc.
7370 MacArthur Blvd.
Glen Echo, MD 20812
(800) 945-3247

Wild Birds Forever
27212 Highway 189
P.O. Box 4904
Blue Jay, CA 92317
(800) 459-2473

Wild Bird Supplies
4815 Oak Street
Crystal Lake, IL 60012
(815) 455-4020
Seed, feed, feeders, houses

Wild Birds Unlimited
11711 N. College Ave., Suite 146
Carmel, IN 46032
(317) 571-7100

APPENDIX H

Bird Societies

American Birding Association
Box 6599
Colorado Springs, CO 80934
(800) 835-2473

National Audubon Society
700 Broadway
New York, NY 10003
(212) 979-3000

National Audubon Society
Sanctuary Department
Lucille Brock
lbrock@audubon.org

Niobrara Valley Preserve
Route 1, Box 348
Johnstown, NE 69214
(402) 722-4440
E-mail: trodehnal@tnc.org

North American Bluebird Society
P.O. Box 74
Darlington, WI 53530

Roger Tory Peterson Institute
110 Marvin Parkway
Jamestown, NY 14701
(716) 665-BIRD

The Purple Martin Conservation Association
Box 178
Edinboro, PA 16412
E-mail: pmca@edinboro.edu

APPENDIX I

Bird Sanctuaries

Appleton-Whittell Research Sanctuary
HC1, Box 44
Elgin, AZ 85611
(520) 455-5522

Audubon Center in Greenwich and Fairchild Wildflower Garden
613 Riversville Road
Greenwich, CT 06831
(203) 869-5272

Audubon Center of the Northwoods
Route 1, Box 288
Sandstone, MN 55072
(320) 245-2648

Aullwood Audubon Center and Farm
1000 Aullwood Road
Dayton, OH 45414
(937) 890-7360

Bent of the River Sanctuary
Sanctuary Department
93 West Cornwall Road
Sharon, CT 06069
(860) 364-0048

Bobelaine Sanctuary
Sacramento Audubon Society
Laurel Ave.
Yuba City, CA 95695
(530) 661-6061

Borestone Mountain Sanctuary
P.O. Box 524
Dover-Foxcroft, ME 04426

Briarbush Sanctuary
1212 Edge Hill Rd.
Adington, PA 19001
(215) 887-6603

Edward M. Brigham II - Alkali Lake Sanctuary
2646 90th Ave. SE
Spiritwood, ND 58481
(701) 252-3822

Clyde E. Buckley Sanctuary
1305 Germany Road
Frankfort, KY 40601
(859) 873-5711

Buttercup Wildlife Sanctuary
Wildlife Sanctuary
Sharon, CT 06069
(860) 364-0057

Constitution Marsh Sanctuary
RFD 2 Route 9D
Garrison, NY 10524
(845) 265-2601

Corkscrew Swamp Sanctuary
375 Sanctuary Road
West Naples, FL 33964
(941) 348-9151

Cowpens Key Tavernier Science Center Staff
115 Indian Mound Trail
Tavernier, FL 33070
(305) 852-5092

Dauphin Island Sanctuary
109 Bienville Blvd.
Dauphin Island, AL 36528
(251) 861-6992

Randall Davey Center
P.O. Box 9314
Santa Fe, NM 87504
(505) 983-4609

Francis Beidler Forest Sanctuary
336 Sanctuary Road
Harleyville, SC 29448
(843) 462-2150

Great Salt Lake Sanctuary
549 Cortez Street
Salt Lake City, UT 84103
(801) 355-8110

Guilford Salt Meadows Sanctuary
N2384 Hunt Hill Rd.
Sarona, WI 54870
(715) 635-6543

Hunt Hill Sanctuary
RR 1 Box 285, Audubon Road
Sarona, WI 54870
(715) 635-6543

Lake Okeechobee Sanctuary/Ordway-Whittell Kissimmee Prairie Sanctuary
100 Riverwoods Circle
Lorida, FL 33857

Maine Coastal Islands Sanctuary
12 Audubon Road
Bremen, ME 04551

Emily W. Miles Wildlife Sanctuary
95 West Cornwall Road
Sharon, CT 06069
(860) 364-0057

Niobrara Valley Preserve
Route 1, Box 348
Johnstown, NE 69214
(402) 722-4440
E-mail: trodehnal@tnc.org

North Carolina Coastal Islands Sanctuary
720 Market St.
Wilmington, NC 28401

Pine Island Sanctuary
P.O. Box 174
Poplar Branch, NC 27965
(252) 453-4839

Paul J. Rainey Wildlife Sanctuary
10149 Richard Rd.
Abbeville, LA 70510-9216

RamsHorn-Livingston Sanctuary
c/o Scenic Hudson
9 Vassar St.
Poughkeepsie, NY 12601
(845) 473-4440

Richardson Bay Wildlife Sanctuary and Whittell Education Center
National Audubon Nature Education Center
376 Greenwood Beach Road
Tiburon, CA 94920
(415) 388-2524

Lillian Annette Rowe Sanctuary
44450 Elm Island Rd.
Gibbon, NE 68840
(308) 468-5282

Sabal Palm Grove Sanctuary
P.O. Box 5052
Brownsville, TX 78523
(956) 541-8034

Schlitz Audubon Center
1111 East Brown Deer Road
Milwaukee, WI 53217
(414) 352-2880

Sharon Audubon Center
325 Cornwall Bridge Road
Sharon, CT 06069
(860) 364-0520

Starr Ranch Sanctuary
Resident Manager
100 Bell Canyon Road
Trabuco Canyon, CA 92679
(949) 858-0309

Tampa Bay Sanctuary
410 Ware Boulevard, Suite 500
Tampa, FL 33619
(813) 623-6826

Tenmile Creek Sanctuary
P.O. Box 496
Yachats, OR 97498
(541-547-4227

Texas Coastal Islands Sanctuary
205 N. Carrizo St.
Corpus Christi, TX 78401
(361) 884-2634

Todd Wildlife Sanctuary
c/o Maine Audubon Society
20 Gilslad Farm Rd.
Falmouth, ME 04105
(207) 563-8280

Paul L. Wattis Sanctuary
555 Audubon Place
Sacramento, CA 95825
(916) 481-5440

Williams Sisters Ranch Sanctuary
555 Audubon Place
Sacramento, CA 95825
(916) 481-5440

APPENDIX J

All About Audubon

National Audubon Society
700 Broadway
New York, NY 10003-9562
(212) 979-3000
Fax: (212) 979-3188

Mission

The mission of the National Audubon Society is to conserve and restore natural ecosystems, focusing on birds, other wildlife and their habitats, for the benefit of humanity and the earth's biological diversity.Through this work, Audubon strives to create a culture of conservation that supports this conservation and restoration.

Statistics

- 550,000 members
- 516 chapters in the United States
- 20,000 members of the Activist Network
- 300 scientists, educators, sanctuary managers, regional and state directors, government affairs specialists, and other professional staff

History

The National Audubon Society was founded in 1886 by George Bird Grinnell, named for naturalist and wildlife painter John James Audubon (1785–1851), and incorporated as a national organization in 1905.

High-Priority Campaigns and Key Legislative Priorities

- Restoring the Everglades of Florida
- Protecting corridors for migratory birds with the Birds in the Balance program
- Preserving wetlands through reauthorization of the Clean Water Act
- Lobbying to reauthorize the Endangered Species Act
- Securing the integrity of the Adirondacks of New York and the forests of the Northeast
- Protecting the ancient forests of the Pacific Northwest
- Defending marine wildlife through the Living Oceans program
- Promoting a responsible U.S. population policy
- Working for environmental justice in urban and international forums
- Restoring water flows to enhance wildlife of the Platte River system
- Preserving whole ecosystems through Audubon sanctuaries

Publications

- *Audubon Magazine* is a bimonthly forum for discussion of the world's emerging environmental agenda.
- *Audubon Adventures* is published seven times a year for children and educators.
- Activist fact sheets, brochures, toolkits, videos and slide shows.

Audubon Productions

National Audubon Society Productions (NASP) reaches out to both active and latent environmentalists using mass media. NASP produces Audubon TV specials for TBS Superstation, programs for the Disney Channel, TV movies, music videos, interactive multimedia software, specialty videos, and companion books and software on issues which support the Audubon mission. Also in development are feature films, a weekly talk show, children's programming, the *How To Make A Difference* video series, and IMAX films.

There is such a thing as an independent Audubon Society and these are not affiliated with the National Audubon Society.

Connecticut Audubon Society
2325 Burr Street
Fairfield, CT 06430
(203) 259-6305
Fax (203) 254-7673

Federation of New York State Bird Clubs
P.O. Box 440
Loch Sheldrake, NY 12759

Maine Audubon Society Gilsland Farm Road
20 Gilsland Farm Rd.
Falmouth, ME 04105
(207) 781-2330

Maryland Ornithological Society
Cylburn Mansion
4915 Greenspring Avenue
Baltimore, MD 21209
(800) 823-0050

New Jersey Audubon Society
Box 125
Franklin Lakes, NJ 07417
(201) 891-1211
Fax (201) 891-2185

State Birding Associations Connecticut Ornithological Association
314 Unquowa Road
Fairfield, CT 06430

A very important source:
Cornell Laboratory of Ornithology, Division of Visual Services
159 Sapsucker Woods Road
Ithaca, NY 14850
(607) 254-2450

APPENDIX K

State Birds

Alabama	Northern flicker
Alaska	Willow ptarmigan
Arizona	Cactus wren
Arkansas	Northern mockingbird
California	California quail
Colorado	Lark bunting
Connecticut	American robin
Delaware	Blue hen chicken
District of Columbia	Wood thrush
Florida	Northern mockinghird
Georgia	Brown thrasher
Hawaii	Nene
Idaho	Mountain bluebird
Illinois	Northern cardinal
Indiana	Northern cardinal
Iowa	American goldfinch
Kansas	Western meadowlark
Kentucky	Northern cardinal
Louisiana	Brown pelican
Maine	Black-capped chickadee
Maryland	Northern ("Baltimore") oriole
Massachusetts	Black-capped chickadee
Michigan	American robin
Minnesota	Common loon

Mississippi	Northern mockingbird
Missouri	Eastern bluebird
Montana	Western meadowlark
Nebraska	Western meadowlark
Nevada	Mountain bluebird
New Hampshire	Purple finch
New Jersey	American goldfinch
New Mexico	Greater roadrunner
New York	Eastern bluebird
North Carolina	Northern cardinal
North Dakota	Western meadowlark
Ohio	Northern cardinal
Oklahoma	Scissor-tailed flycatcher
Oregon	Western meadowlark
Pennsylvania	Ruffled grouse
Rhode Island	Rhode Island red chicken
South Carolina	Carolina wren
South Dakota	Ring-necked pheasant
Tennessee	Northern mockingbird
Texas	Northern mockingbird
Utah	California gull
Vermont	Hermit thrust
Virginia	Northern cardinal
Washington	American goldfinch
West Virginia	Northern cardinal
Wisconsin	American robin
Wyoming	Western meadowlark

APPENDIX L

Cavity-Nesting Birds

Black-bellied whistling duck
Red-bellied woodpecker
Mexican chickadee
Wood duck
Golden-fronted woodpecker
Mountain chickadee
Common goldeneye
Gila woodpecker
Gray-headed chickadee
Barrow's goldeneye
Red-headed woodpecker
Boreal chickadee
Bufflehead
Acorn woodpecker
Chestnut-backed chickadee
Hooded merganser
Lewis' woodpecker
Tufted titmouse
Common merganser
Yellow-bellied sapsucker
Plain titmouse
Turkey vulture
Williamson's sapsucker

Bridled titmouse
Black vulture
Hairy woodpecker
White-breasted nuthatch
Peregrine falcon*
Downy woodpecker
Red-breasted nuthatch
Merlin
Ladder-backed woodpecker
Brown-headed nuthatch
American kestrel
Nuttall's woodpecker
Pygmy nuthatch
Barn owl
Arizona woodpecker
Brown creeper
Screech owl
Red-cockaded woodpecker
House wren
Whiskered owl
White-headed woodpecker
Brown-throated wren
Flammulated owl
Black-backed three-toed woodpecker
Winter wren
Hawk owl
Northern three-toed woodpecker
Bewick's wren
Pygmy owl
Ivory-billed woodpecker*
Carolina wren
Ferruginous owl

Sulphur-bellied flycatcher
Eastern bluebird
Elf owl
Great crested flycatcher
Western bluebird
Barred owl
Wied's crested flycatcher
Mountain bluebird
Spotted owl
Ash-throated flycatcher
Starling
Boreal owl
Olivaceous flycatcher
Crested myna
Saw-whet owl
Western flycatcher
Prothonotary warbler
Chimney swift
Violet-green swallow
Lucy's warbler
Vaux's swift
Tree swallow
House sparrow
Coppery-tailed trogon
Purple martin
European tree sparrow
Common flicker
Black-capped chickadee
Pileated woodpecker
Carolina chickadee

**Threatened or endangered species*

APPENDIX M

Possible Life Spans of North American Birds

Eastern bluebird	3–6 years
Cardinal	4–13 years
Black-capped chickadee	5–12 years
Gray catbird	4–10 years
Mourning dove	5–10 years
House finch	6–10 years
Purple finch	6–12 years
Goldfinch	4–8 years
Evening grosbeak	4 years
Ruby-throated hummingbird	4–12 years
Blue jay	5–15 years
Dark-eyed junco	3–10 years
Purple martin	4–8 years
Mockingbird	4–12 years
White-breasted nuthatch	5–9 years
Baltimore oriole	6–8 years
Phoebe	2–9 years
House sparrow	13 years
Starling	5–16 years
Barn swallow	5–8 years
Scarlet tanager	3–9 years
Tufted titmouse	3–12 years
Rufous-sided towhee	7–10 years
Cedar waxwing	3–7 years

Downy woodpecker	4–10 years
House wren	5–7 years
Winter wren	$5\frac{3}{4}$ years
Brown thrasher	4–12 years
American robin	4–$11\frac{1}{2}$ years
Screech wwl	6–13 years
Eastern kingbird	3–8 years
Common grackle	4–16 years
Common flicker	5–$12\frac{1}{2}$ years
Common crow	6–14 years
Brown-headed cowbird	5–$13\frac{1}{2}$ years
Red-winged blackbird	4–$14\frac{1}{2}$ years

Ages are from official banding records of birds from files of the U.S. Fish and Wildlife Service, Washington, D.C.

Note: Hummingbirds, warblers, and other very small birds probably live only a year or two.